Water, Rivers and Creeks

Water, Rivers and Creeks

Luna B. Leopold

UNIVERSITY OF CALIFORNIA, BERKELEY

University Science Books
Sausalito, California

University Science Books
55D Gate Five Road
Sausalito, CA 94965
Fax: (415) 332-5393

Designer: Robert Ishi
Illustrators: John and Judy Waller
Compositor: Wilsted & Taylor Publishing Services
Printer & Binder: Maple-Vail Book Manufacturing Group

This book is printed on acid-free paper. The typeface is Sabon.

Library of Congress Cataloging-in-Publication Data

Leopold, Luna Bergere, 1915–
        Water, rivers, and creeks / by Luna Leopold.
              p.   cm.
        Includes bibliographical references and index.
        ISBN 0-935702-98-9
        1. Water.   I. Title
GB671.L43   1997
551.48—dc21   97-9507
                                                          CIP

Printed in the United States of America
10   9   8   7   6   5   4   3   2   1

To
Madelyn and Claude
Niki and Bruce
Carrie and Rett

Contents

Preface

In the last decades of the 20th century the rate of loss of the world's natural resources has increased. Included in this loss are the clearing of forests both on tropical and subhumid land masses, a precipitous loss of fisheries in the oceans and in anadromous species, and increased pollution of rivers and lakes on which a growing population depends. Even in the United States where a well-educated citizenry is well informed, environmental gains have been under attack, with the aim of furthering development and increasing profits. The trend is particularly worrisome because the assault stresses the resources on which all peoples of the world depend: air, water, soil, and biota.

This trend probably cannot be stopped, but the education of peoples everywhere may slow it down. However small a contribution, this book represents one of the ways people can be led to see the larger picture of their dependence on the natural environment. The better we understand the workings of the biota and the landscape, the more likely we are to learn to appreciate and value the environment.

An ecosystem is complicated, and few writers are so versed in both the physical and biologic elements that a really exhaustive treatment can be given. Because I am not so versed, a simple book such as this one cannot do everything that would ideally be required. It would be better if this volume dealt with the biotic as well as with the physical aspects of rivers and waters; unfortunately, that is not within my capability.

This book is an expanded and a reorganized version of an earlier book, *Water—A Primer*, published in 1974 by W. H. Freeman Company. That book has been out of print for many years and a new edition has been suggested.

I am greatly indebted to Michael Church, David Freyberg, David

Dawdy, and James Kirchner for very helpful reviews of the manuscript, for they pointed out many items where improvement was necessary. These scientists have added greatly to the technical and the editorial contents of this work.

The Oxford University Press has permitted me to quote from *Round River* by Aldo Leopold. My thanks go to Susan Noble of Cora, Wyoming, for assistance in manuscript preparation.

LBL 1997
Pinedale, Wyoming

Foreword

One of the marvels of early Wisconsin was the Round River, a river that flowed into itself, and thus sped around and around in a never-ending circuit. Paul Bunyan discovered it, and the Bunyan saga tells how he floated many a log down its restless waters.

No one has suspected Paul of speaking in parables, yet in this instance he did ... The current is the stream of energy which flows out of the soil into plants, thence into animals, thence back into the soil in a never-ending circuit of life.

We of the genus Homo ride the logs that float down the Round River, and by a little judicious "burling" we have learned to guide their direction and speed. This feat entitles us to the specific appellation sapiens. The technique of burling is called economics, the remembering of old routes is called history, the selection of new ones is called statesmanship, the conversation about oncoming riffles and rapids is called politics. Some of the crew aspire to burl not only their own logs, but the whole flotilla as well. This collective bargaining with nature is called national planning.

To learn the hydrology of the biotic stream we must think at right angles to evolution and examine the collective behavior of biotic materials ... Ecology is the science that attempts this feat of thinking in a plane perpendicular to Darwin.

Aldo Leopold
in *Round River*, 1953
Oxford University Press

Water, Rivers and Creeks

I

Hydrology and Morphology

Precipitation

Water circulates from earth to atmosphere to earth

In the Middle Ages people believed that the water in rivers flowed magically from the center of the earth. Late in the seventeenth century Edmond Halley, the famous English astronomer, added up the amount of water flowing in rivers to the Mediterranean Sea and found it to be approximately equal to the amount of water falling as rain and snow on the area drained by the same rivers. At nearly the same time, the Frenchman Claude Perrault measured the flow of the upper Seine and found it to be only approximately one-sixth of the precipitation computed to fall on the river basin. He correctly surmised that losses caused by evaporation and infiltration might account for the difference. These are the earliest known instances of anyone having correctly reasoned that precipitation feeds lakes, rivers, and springs. This idea was very advanced for the time. Today, numerous river-measuring stations permit these kinds of comparisons and calculations to be made accurately in many parts of the world.

Water is constantly exchanged between the earth and the atmosphere. This exchange is accomplished by the heat of the sun and the pull of gravity. Water evaporates from wet ground, the leaves of growing plants, lakes, reservoirs and the ocean. It is carried in the air as water vapor. When water vapor condenses it changes from a gas to a liquid and falls as the rain that feeds the rivers and lakes. Rivers carry water to the ocean. Evaporation from land and ocean puts water back in the atmosphere, and this exchange goes on continually: Water goes from earth to atmosphere to earth. The exchange of water between earth and atmosphere is the hydrologic cycle—hydro means having to do with water, *logos* is a Greek word meaning knowledge of. Hydrology is the study or knowledge of water.

3

Rain and snow

A person sitting on a screened porch sipping an iced drink on a hot summer day notices that the outside of the glass gets wet and puts the glass on a coaster to protect the table top. The glass does not leak, so the droplets of water on its outside must have come from the air. The water condenses on the glass from water vapor in the air. When water vapor is a gas mixed with air, it is invisible. The skin can sense the presence of large amounts of water vapor, and when it does the day is said to be "muggy."

The amount of water vapor the air can carry without loss by condensation depends on the air temperature. The higher the temperature, the more vapor the air can carry. When moist air cools sufficiently, there is too much water for the air to hold as vapor. Some vapor changes to liquid water, forming droplets that fall of their weight. The ice in the cold drink cooled the air and condensed the vapor on the outside of the glass. This is the basic process by which rain forms in the atmosphere.

Snow forms by a similar process: The temperature is so low that the water freezes when the vapor condenses. The hoarfrost that forms on the inside of a window pane on a cold winter day is an analogous process, as the water vapor in the room condenses as ice on the cold windowpane.

What causes the atmosphere to cool so that vapor condenses as rain or snow? The principal cause is the lifting of warm air to higher and cooler altitudes. Around the earth is a layer of air, or atmosphere, that thins from the ground upward. Its pressure is greater at ground level than it is 5 miles above ground level because the layer is 5 miles thicker. When air is lifted up to an altitude where the layer of atmosphere above it is thinner, it expands because the pressure on it is less. Expansion cools the air by allowing its molecules to spread farther apart, thus reducing the frequency of their collision. Bug bombs and other kinds of metal cans containing compressed gas get cold when the pressure is released and the gas is allowed to escape. The principle is the same with rising water vapor: as it expands upward, it cools.

If cooling is sufficient, the vapor condenses as droplets of water and these droplets form rain. The condensation is helped by the presence of small particles of dust or salt that are ever-present in the air.

The lifting itself comes about in two principal ways. First, winds that blow toward hills or mountains are forced to rise over the obstacle. The rising air cools, as previously explained. This is a common cause of rain and snow in mountainous terrain. Second, when a mass of warm or light air meets a cold and heavy mass of air, the lighter air rises over the heavier air. In this situation the cold and heavy air acts like the mountain; it is an obstacle over which the warmer air must rise.

There is a third way in which air rises to levels where condensation of moisture may occur. Air close to a warm ground surface is heated from below just as water in a teakettle is heated by the flame on the stove. The heated air expands, becomes lighter, and rises. This is the cause of most late afternoon thunderstorms that occur on hot midsummer days.

Clouds are composed of many droplets of ice or condensed water. The wispy clouds at high levels are composed of small crystals of ice, but dark threatening storm clouds and fleecy ones are made up of water droplets. The color of clouds depends on the quantity and type of light reflected from the cloud. The light reflected from clouds generally is white.

Because clouds and rain are closely related to hydrology, a brief description of weather processes has been included here. Meteorology, the study of weather, is an earth science, and all the sciences that deal with the earth are closely related to one another.

Sources of moisture in the air

Rainfall, snowfall, sleet, and hail are collectively known as precipitation, a word derived from Latin, meaning to fall headlong. The word rainfall is also used in the general sense to mean precipitation.

Where does most of the moisture that falls from the clouds as rain come from? Water evaporates from the ground surface, from vegetation, from all open bodies of water, such as lakes and rivers, and, of course, from the ocean. Large amounts of water are discharged to the atmosphere by the process of transpiration. For example, an acre of corn gives off to the air approximately 11,000 to 15,000 liters of water each day. A large oak tree gives off approximately 150,000 liters per year. This water is first taken up by the roots from the soil, moves up the trunk as sap, and emerges from the plant through thousands of small holes on the under side of every leaf.

Transpiration from plants is one of the important sources of water vapor in the air and often produces more vapor than does evaporation from land surface, lakes, and streams. However, the most important source of moisture in the air is evaporation from the oceans, particularly those parts of the ocean that lie in the warm parts of the earth.

For this reason, the rain that falls on cities in the central United States is probably largely composed of particles of water that were evaporated from the ocean near the equator or from the Gulf of Mexico. Only a relatively small part was evaporated or transpired from rivers, lakes, and plants in the vicinity of the rainfall. Winds in the upper air carry moisture long distances from the oceans where evaporation is great.

The heat required to change the water from liquid to vapor in the familiar process known as evaporation has already been described. The air carries away the heat with the vapor, and the heat is given up when the vapor condenses to form clouds. Thus the earth's atmosphere is a vast heat engine powered by the sun. Through the energy provided by the sun, water evaporates from the land and ocean, is carried as vapor in the air, falls somewhere as rain or snow, and returns to the ocean or to the land again to go through the same process.

Although this universal truth was forgotten in the Dark Ages, the ancients may have had some appreciation of this grand cycle. According to the Bible, "All the rivers run into the sea, yet the sea is never full; unto the place from whence the rivers come thither they return again."

As the water circulates over the earth through this grand cycle, usable water is accessible only while it is on the land surface or in the ground.

Rainfall amounts

Because water on the earth derives from precipitation, it is useful to have in mind a conception of the quantities involved, first by noting some amounts of precipitation in various climates. Consider the annual values of precipitation in the continental United States.

Most eastern states receive from 1,000 to 1,270 mm annually. Washington, D.C., for example, experiences about 1,000 mm per year. The Appalachian Mountains receive higher amounts, especially in northern Georgia and western South Carolina, where 2,000 mm per year is common.

The midwestern states receive 750 to 1,000 annually. Chicago gets 800 mm, Kansas City 900 mm, and Oklahoma City 790 mm.

Made famous by John Wesley Powell, Bernard De Voto and Wallace Stegner, the area west of the 100th meridian is known as *The West*, where there is more land than water, and annual precipitation totals are sharply lower. Most nonmountainous areas of the west but east of California's Sierra Nevada range receive 500 mm or less of rainfall per year. Mountain tops receive as much as 900 mm in some places, but the values in valley areas range from 380 to 500 mm. Denver receives 350 mm, as does Santa Fe. Salt Lake City gets 400 mm, but Wendover, Utah, on the western border of Great Salt Lake, receives only 130 mm.

As an exception to this low precipitation in the west, the Sierra Nevada mountain tops receive from 1,500 to 1,750 mm and coastal California gets from 500 to more than 2,500 mm.

In general, the regions west of the 100th meridian require irrigation for agriculture. Agricultural water usage far exceeds that used by cities and by industry. As will be seen in the discussion of water use, irrigated agriculture constitutes as much as 85 percent of all the water used in the United States.

Irrigation is now practiced in many areas of the eastern United States, even where the annual precipitation is 900 mm. This practice results from the desire to mitigate the effects of dry seasons or dry periods.

Successful dry farming requires 750 mm or more of precipitation annually. Most of the land areas of the western states receive less than that amount.

It is also important to note that there is a shift in the season of greatest precipitation as one progresses eastward across the United States. California has a climate called Mediterranean, because, like Spain, Italy, and Greece, the rainy season occurs in winter and the summer is dry. Much of California receives less than 50 mm of rain in the 6 month period from April to September.

Somewhat to the east of the Mediterranean climate, there is a wide area in which two rainy seasons exist: frontal winter storms and summer thunderstorms. This two-period timing of precipitation characterizes eastern Arizona, New Mexico, and west Texas. Still farther to the east, Louisiana receives much of its rain in summer, mostly from thunderstorms.

In the northern tier of states, where snowfall contributes an important part of the annual precipitation, annual rainfall is distributed more or less uniformly in spring, summer and fall, with the winter contributing less rain but more snow than the other seasons. Most of the great floods are caused by rainfall on wet or frozen ground, not by snowmelt.

Rainfall intensity

Thunderstorm rains are an important cause of floods in small areas and are important in erosion processes. Therefore, a discusssion of rainfall intensity is in order. Maximum recorded values of rainfall in 24 hours are in the range of 100 to 500 mm in northern California, western Washington, and Oregon, but, only 50 to 100 mm in the eastern parts of those states. Twenty-four hour values may be 250 to 500 mm in Texas, Iowa, western Carolinas, and Florida. One-hour values of rainfall ranging from 75 to 130 mm have been recorded in Texas, Florida, and eastern North Carolina. The eastern states experience an average of from 150 to 200 mm in 24 hours.

Great floods often result from excessive rain continuing over several days. The storms of 1993 in the Midwest broke most previous records. Some locations in Minnesota received more than 177 mm in one day and in New London, Iowa, 165 mm fell in 15 minutes. During an intense thunderstorm, I have experienced rain falling at the rate of 175 mm per hour for a few minutes. One has the feeling that it is impossible to breathe.

Although somewhat outdated, good maps of climatic elements, precipitation, snow, frost, and temperature, can be found in *Climate and Man*, the 1941 Yearbook of Agriculture, Government Printing Office, Washington D.C., and in *World Survey of Climatology*. Another complete compilation is in the two volumes of *Climates of the States*, 1974.

Infiltration

The water that falls on the earth is disposed of in three ways. It evaporates into the air, it sinks into the ground, or it runs off the surface of the ground.

That part of the hydrologic cycle that is of most concern to the human population is water on and in the land. Water on the land surface is visible in lakes, ponds, rivers, and creeks or surface water. What is not seen is the important water that is out of sight—called groundwater. It is convenient to refer to surface and groundwater separately in describing the location of the water, even though they are not different kinds of water. Both come from precipitation. A third type of water flow is also unseen—that part that is infiltrated into the ground.

During a heavy rainstorm, water may flow down the gutter and the ground gets wet and remains wet or at least damp for days, but during light rains, little or no water runs in the gutters and the ground seems dry in minutes after the rain. These observations lead to the conclusion that when rain strikes the ground, part of it sinks into the soil and part runs off the surface to gutters or to natural channels. What happens to each of these parts of the total rainfall will be discussed separately.

The surface of the soil has often been compared to a blotter. It could be more accurately compared to a sieve made of a fine mesh. If such a sieve is held under the faucet when the water is slowly coming out of the tap, all the water flows through the screen. If the water flow is increased, the bowl of the sieve fills up and finally overflows because the water cannot flow through the fine holes of the screen as fast as it comes out of the faucet.

If the experiment is performed with another sieve having larger holes in the mesh, it is clear that even at maximum water flow, the screen can pass all the water and the bowl does not overflow. It can be seen that the rate at which the water can be passed through the screen depends on the size of the holes or openings. Further, the faster the water falls on the screen, the larger will be the amount that does not flow through the sieve but overflows the sides instead.

A somewhat similar effect can be seen when rain falls on the soil surface. In effect, there are many very small holes or spaces between the grains of sand or the particles of dirt on the earth's surface. Therefore, the soil acts as a screen or sieve. The larger the particles of dirt, sand, or gravel that make up the ground surface, the larger are the holes or spaces in between the particles and the more the surface acts like a sieve mesh with large openings.

When rain falls rapidly on a sandy or gravelly surface, all of the water goes through the sieve-like openings into the ground. When rain falls rapidly on a clay or fine-grained soil, however, the rate of passage through the smaller soil spaces is lower, and the rain that cannot get through the holes flows over the ground as a sheet of water. This surface flow corresponds to the water that overflows the bowl of the sieve when the faucet is flowing strongly. The part of the rainfall that does not infiltrate or pass into the soil flows over the earth's surface to a gully or channel and is surface runoff.

The rate of infiltration depends principally on two factors: the characteristics of the soil material and the type and density of vegetation growing or lying on the soil surface. Sandy soils tend to have higher infiltration rates than fine-grained soils, such as silty or clay loams, because there are larger spaces between the grains. However, even silty loams may have relatively high rates of infiltration if there is a large amount of organic material in the surface horizons.

Infiltration rate is stated in units of centimeters or millimeters per hour, the same unit used to describe the rate of rainfall. One millimeter of rain falling on a unit area of ground surface in one hour means that one hour after the beginning of rainfall, the water standing in a pan is 1 mm deep, spread across the bottom of the pan. Whether the pan is small or large, the water depth is still 1 mm, and thus mm per hour is a unit that is independent of area.

Infiltration rate refers to the millimeters of water that pass into the ground surface per unit of time. If rain falls on the soil's surface at a rate of 1 cm per hour and the infiltration rate is ¼ cm per hour, the remaining ¾ cm per hour runs off the surface because it has not been infiltrated.

Infiltration rate is higher when the soil is dry and lower after it is wetted. During a rainstorm, the infiltration rate decreases with the passage of time and finally assumes a uniform and minimum value. The infiltration rate decreases as rainfall continues for two principal reasons. First, wetting the soil causes granules of clay or silt to expand, thus closing some of the pore space between granules. Second, the film of water that surrounds each grain is more or less continuous and forms a three-dimensional network of interconnected veins of water. The liquid flows downward through the net but the rate of downward movement decreases for a variety of reasons, including the lower permeability due to the reduced frequency of root casts, animal burrows, and the pressure of the overburden.

Some soils are hydrophobic, or not easily wetted. They resist water penetration at the beginning of a rain. This is a situation common along the margin of a dusty road.

During a dry period, the drainage of the water out of the soil and the loss to the air by evaporation cause the infiltration rate to change, increasing to its dry-soil value so that when another rain begins, the infiltration rate is again high at the beginning and decreases with time.

Normal infiltration rates vary around 25 mm per hour but may be much greater in well-vegetated areas where there is a layer of duff or organic litter on the soil surface. Three infiltration curves (which plot infiltration rate as a function of time) are shown in Figure 1. The shape

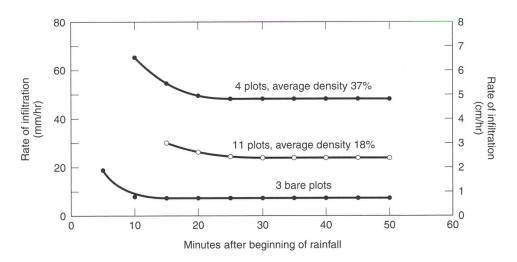

Figure 1   Infiltration rate showing the effect of vegetative density. The curves show the averages for 18 experiments on wet clay loam soil; vegetation is desert shrub. Field experiments were conducted near Roswell, New Mexico. (Adapted from Smith and Leopold, *Soil Science*, LIII, 1942, 195–204.)

of the curves indicates that the rate decreases as the rain continues. The figure also shows the effect of vegetative density. The top curve applies to experimental plots with 37 percent of the surface covered by grass or other plants. The bottom curve applies to plots that were bare of any grass. The vegetated surface, though less than half covered with grass, had a minimum infiltration rate of 48 mm per hour, whereas the bare plots were infiltrated at a rate of only 8 mm per hour.

It is apparent that more of the precipitation will get into the soil if the surface is vegetated. Thus less water will run off the ground surface into rills or channels. Vegetation reduces surface runoff and increases the amount of water that could potentially accumulate as stored groundwater.

Evaporation

When rain falls the wetted surfaces of leaves, stems, soil, and rocks immediately begin losing water by evaporation. The amount that neither infiltrates nor contributes to surface runoff is called interception. In heavily vegetated areas, falling rain is initially stored on the branches and stems of plants, and further rain will cause water to fall off these surfaces, finally reaching the soil.

The quantity of intercepted water can be an important component because all of it returns to the air and does not contribute to surface flow, groundwater, or soil moisture. The amount so returned by evaporation varies from one type of vegetation to another. In a deciduous forest and mature crops, 10 to 30 percent of the annual rainfall is evaporated from interception.

Evaporation from open water bodies, lakes, reservoirs, and ponds, is appreciable. In the semiarid areas and mountains, the amount evaporated is much larger than the precipitation received on the evaporating surface. For example, in north central New Mexico where at elevations of 2,500 m the annual precipitation is 350 mm, the annual evaporation from reservoirs and lakes is 1,200 to 1,500 mm. In southern and southwestern Texas the annual evaporation from reservoirs is 1,750 to 2,030 mm. These sample values indicate the significance of water lost from large irrigation reservoirs that can be so important to the economy of irrigated landscapes.

In the eastern United States, where the annual precipitation is 890 to 1,150 mm, the evaporation losses from open water bodies range from 750 to 1,000 mm, but the cumulative areas of lakes and reservoirs are smaller and less important than in the lower rainfall areas of the West.

Transpiration

Transpiration is a larger component in the water cycle than is evaporation. Transpiration is the exudation by which all plants—trees, shrubs, and grasses—expel water from the leaves as part of the photosynthetic process. The plants draw water into the roots from soil moisture, obtaining at the same time the dissolved materials needed for growth. The combination of transpiration and evaporation involves the return to the atmosphere of 70 percent of the precipitation that falls on the land. Only 30 percent of the precipitation appears as surface streamflow. Because plants imbibe water from soil moisture, the process of infiltration is very important.

Thus the three part division of precipitation is clear. The water that falls is divided and proceeds through three routes—evaporation, infiltration, and surface runoff. The first is the smallest. And although runoff is important, the majority of the water received at the ground surface infiltrates, a large proportion of which is taken up by plants through transpiration and returned as water vapor to the atmosphere.

Movement of water within the soil

Anyone who has had occasion to dig in the garden soon after a rain probably found that the soil was wet for several inches down from the surface but dry below that. Two forces, capillarity and gravity, move water downward in the soil.

Moisture moves downward because it is pulled down from below. The pull is rather like that in the wick of a kerosene lamp or a candle. If a piece of dry string is placed so that one end is in a pan of water and the other end hangs over the side with its tip lower than the level of the water in the pan, the water gradually rises up the string, wetting the whole length, and drips off the tip. This is an example of the principle of capillary action. A drop of water tends to spread out in a thin film over very small particles such as those in the cloth of the wick or the particles of soil. Capillarity is the tendency of a liquid to cling to the surface of a solid material, and this tendency may draw the liquid up, against the pull of gravity, as in the case of a candle wick. Similarly, capillarity may draw water downward into the dry soil below the wet portion.

Conversely, when the particles of soil are coarse, that is, they consist of large sand grains or small pebbles, water is pulled by gravity and tends to flow downward more or less freely through the pore spaces. Similarly, water may flow downward through holes made by worms or left by decayed roots.

Consider what happens to moisture in a deep soil. The soil material lying below the land surface is usually filled partly with water and partly with air. When rainfall infiltrates into the soil, it fills the open spaces and temporarily replaces the air. Water in the larger open spaces, like those between coarse sand particles, moves downward more rapidly than the water held in the smaller spaces.

A sandy soil drains rapidly after a heavy rainfall, and after 2 or 3 days only the capillary water is left clinging as a film around the individual soil particles. After gravity has drained the water out of the larger openings, capillary moisture remains like the water left in washed clothes after wringing. This capillary water can be removed only by drying. At the soil surface, evaporation removes the water. Below the surface but in the uppermost layers of the soil, plant roots take up capillary moisture from the soil and thus the soil is dried. When clothes are hung on the line, the air takes up the moisture not removed by the wringing.

Unless there is more rain, the soil dries until the plants wilt. When the soil's moisture content is very low, soil particles hold on to the moisture so tightly that the plants can no longer pull water from the soil and they die.

Rain falling on a dry soil does not spread uniformly throughout that soil. It wets a certain depth of soil and then, after the rain ends, the downward movement practically stops. The underlying soil remains relatively dry. To wet the underlying soil, more rain must fall.

Thus, downward movement of water in soil may occur by two different processes. The first is a gradual wetting of small particles in which the moisture is pulled by capillary forces from wetted to dry grains. The second is rapid flow under the influence of gravity through the larger openings between particles, as if the holes or openings were pipes.

The capillary water has been pulled downward from grain to grain. The lower limit of this wetting is marked by the change from wetted grains above to dry grains below and can be thought of as a "wetted front" or the bottom part of the wet soil. Further downward movement stops when the wetted front has progressed so far that all the water that has soaked into the soil is held by capillary attraction to the grains; this capillary water can be removed only by drying.

Groundwater

The water table and the aquifer

How deep will water go? To answer this question it is necessary to visualize the nature of the materials making up the near-surface portion of the earth. The earth is like an orange, the skin or rind of which is somewhat different from the inside. The deepest oil wells drilled by man are between 7,500 and 9,000 m deep. This is still an insignificant fraction of the 6,000 km to the center of the earth. Yet an oil well, even at that depth, has penetrated far deeper than the ordinary cracks and joints found in the near-surface rocks.

Water moves underground through pores, holes, and cracks that are often seen in surface rocks. Many of these openings result from weathering; that is, from the chemical and physical processes of disintegration brought about by rain, air, frost, and heat. This weathering of rocks close to the earth's surface importantly involves oxidation, as does the rusting of iron in air. It proceeds as both the chemical alteration of mineral grains and physical disintegration. Chemical changes within the minerals are usually accompanied by physical expansion that breaks the mineral grains apart. The weathering of rocks and its products is a large and important subject, a short but broad treatment of which can be found in *Fluvial Processes in Geomorphology* (Leopold et al.).

The soil in which gardens and trees take root is, in fact, derived from hard rock like that found deeper underground. The roadcuts through the hills along a highway reveal the change from surface soil to underlying, broken, cracked, and weathered rock. Below the weathered rock is the hard and solid bedrock. The cracks, seams, and minute spaces between particles of weathered rock become fewer and fewer as depth increases. At some depth these openings are no long present except infrequently, and the movement of water becomes almost impossible.

There is in rocks, however, another kind of hole that allows the seepage of water to great depths. This is the natural pore space between the grains of the rock itself and differs from the fissures discussed previously in that it does not depend on weathering. A common example of rock with natural pore space is sandstone. Many sandstones originated as beach sand on the shore of an ancient ocean. The sand grains later become cemented together to form rock.

Sandstone is one of the principal rocks through which water moves underground. The holes or spaces between the grains of sand permit water to move through the material. When sand becomes cemented by calcium carbonate (lime) or other material to become sandstone, not all the pores between individual grains are filled completely by the cementing material. The cementing material is found mostly where the grains touch, and the spaces between grains remain open. For this reason, sandstone is generally porous, and not only can water pass through the rock, but an appreciable volume of water is required to saturate it. Other porous materials such as gravels were formed in a river bed, then were buried and became part of the bedrock. Such buried gravels may be cemented or may be loose and unconsolidated.

An aquifer is the name for a rock or soil that contains and transmits water and thus is a source for underground water. Aqua means water in Latin, and fer comes from a word meaning to carry. An aquifer is an underground zone or layer that is a relatively good source of water. An aquifer may be an underground zone of gravel or sand, a layer of sandstone, a zone of highly shattered or cracked rock, or a layer of cavernous limestone.

To summarize, underground water may move through the pores of rock or soil material, and through cracks or joints of a rock whether or not the rock itself is porous. The cracks and joints are numerous near the surface and less abundant at greater depths in the earth. As for the depth of occurrence of porous rocks, folding and other mountain-building forces during geologic time have caused materials, such as beach sand turned to sandstone, to become buried many thousands of meters in some places. But underneath these aquifers everywhere at some depth is rock that is impermeable and watertight, because cementation and pressure have closed up the pores.

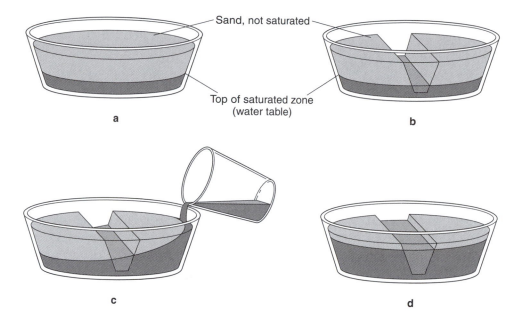

Figure 2 Sand and water in a dishpan demonstrate the relation of the water table to unsaturated soil material.

Thus, water seeping down from the rain-soaked surface will sink so far but no farther, and will collect above the impermeable layer, filling all the pores and cracks of the permeable portions. The top of this saturated zone is the water table.

As a simple analogy, imagine water sprinkled into a dishpan half filled with sand. The water is absorbed in the sand and seeps down through the spaces between sand grains until it reaches the watertight or impermeable bottom of the pan. The sand becomes thoroughly moist before any free water collects at the bottom of the pan. As more water is introduced, the water surface rises gradually until it reaches the surface of the sand.

When there is enough water in the dishpan to saturate the bottom half of the sand, as in Figure 2, the level of the free water surface can be found by poking a hole in the sand with a finger. This hole is partly filled with water, and the water level in the hole is the same as the level of the free water surface throughout the body of the sand. This level, or surface, is the top of the zone of saturation or water table in the porous material. If a V-shaped channel is made across the surface of the bed of sand that is deep enough to expose the surface of the zone of saturation, water will appear in the channel (Figure 2b).

The water table rises until it is exposed in the bottom of the deepest notch or depression in the area, which is usually a river-cut valley. The stream channel is the deepest part of the valley and corresponds to the notch that was cut in the sand in the dishpan. When the water table is high enough to emerge as a free water surface in the stream channel, the water in the channel flows downstream because the channel slopes. Thus water flowing in a river or stream channel long after a rainstorm generally indicates that the water table is high enough to be exposed in the channel. The flow of a river or creek during fair weather is commonly derived from water in the saturated zone of the earth material. In a humid climate, there is enough precipitation to raise the water table high enough for even the small rivulets and creeks to carry water much of the time. In a dry climate, the small channels are dry between rains and only the large, deeply cut river channels carry water all year.

Movement of water in saturated materials

This discussion of downward movement of water and the nature of the groundwater table serves as background to a consideration of the movement of water from one place to another in the ground. For example, when the garden hose is emptied of water and disconnected from the faucet after use, it generally has a good deal of water still in it. To empty it, one end of the hose should be held up in the air and the other end should be allowed to discharge water onto the ground. Water is said to seek its own level. In other words, a water surface tends to become flat; water flows downhill, toward the place where the surface is low. By the same reasoning, unless the water surface slopes, water will not move. In the dishpan example of Figure 2a, the water in the saturated portion of the sand will not move anywhere because the surface of the free water is flat. If a pitcher of water is slowly poured into the sand along one edge of the dishpan, as in Figure 2c, this additional water will temporarily make a mound of water in the sand that will force water to flow sideways until all of it is distributed uniformly throughout the dishpan, as pictured in Figure 2d.

A certain amount of time is required for the mound of water to flatten out and for the water level to be uniform because water flows more slowly through the sand than it would as a sheet of water on the

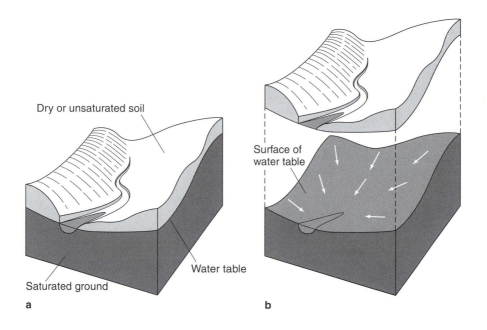

Dry or unsaturated soil

Surface of
water table

Water table

Saturated ground

a

b

Figure 3 Relation of ground surface to water table. A stream channel or rill has water flowing in it where the channel bottom is at a lower elevation than the water table.

surface of the ground. Because of the slow movement of water through the pores, cracks, and minute openings between the grains, the water table in nature is seldom completely flat and horizontal, but rather has an undulating surface. This can be seen in Figure 3, which depicts a small valley with a single stream channel. The figure shows the sides of a block of land lifted out of its position in the earth's surface.

When rain falls on this area, part of the rain seeps downward to the water table and builds a mound, just as did the water that was poured from the pitcher into the sand at the edge of the dishpan. The water in the ground flows downslope toward the stream channel in a similar manner. If the water table is high enough, the water drains out into the stream channel, as in Figure 3a, where the water table is exposed in the small stream channel and appears as water in the stream.

As a further illustration of the water table sloping toward the surface stream, Figure 3b is drawn as though the unsaturated surface of the ground had been lifted up to show the water table in the block of

ground being considered. The following processes that were demonstrated in the dishpan example can be seen in the figure. First, the underground zone of saturation is continuous and has a surface that is
not flat as long as water is moving from the high places toward the lowest place. Second, as indicated by the arrows, groundwater flows
downhill in the direction that represents the steepest slope of the water
surface. In Figure 3b, the lowest point on the surface of the water table
is exposed at the stream or river. The stream carries away all the water
that flows to it, even when large amounts of rain fall and a large mound
of groundwater builds up. After the rain has ceased, groundwater continues to flow toward the stream and gradually the mound of water
flattens out.

Surface streams and rivers continue to flow for a while during long
periods of dry weather, but water levels get progressively lower and
lower as water in the ground is gradually drained away and the water
table approaches a flat or horizontal plane, as it quickly did in the dishpan example. Thus when a farmer says that his ever-flowing brook is
"spring fed," he is using a popular conception to describe the drainage
of groundwater into his brook.

During a rainstorm, a stream may be flowing a moderate amount
of water. The stream will continue to flow for some time after the rain
ceases. However, depending on the size of the stream it will sooner or
later dwindle in flow, only to rise again when another rainstorm comes.

Surface streams are intimately related to water in the ground. The
terms "surface streamflow" and "underground water" apply to the
same water. They merely clarify where the water is at a particular time.
River water and groundwater are the same water, having the same
source.

Field data to describe conditions underground

The situation in the field can best be visualized by considering how one
knows what exists out of sight in the ground. There are many localities
where not merely one but many wells have been drilled. The location
of the wells and the level of water measured in each one is a basic tool
in an investigation of the groundwater resource. A record of the
changes in water level is also important.

Figure 4 presents a hypothetical map of a small basin in which several wells exist and for which there is a record of the water level in dif-

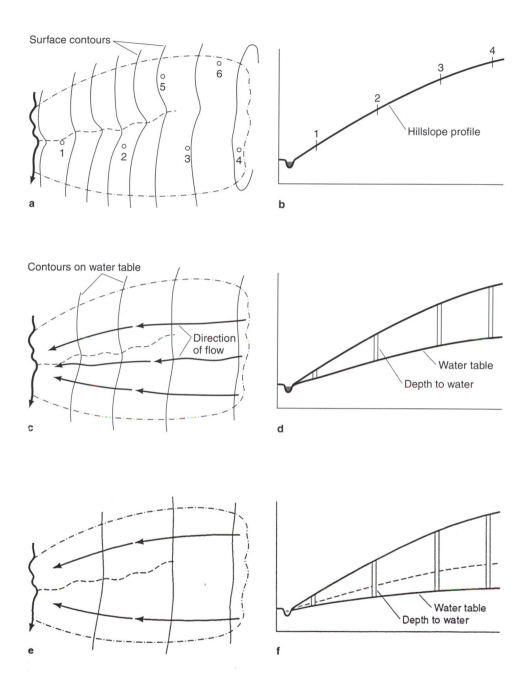

Figure 4 A hypothetical small drainage area showing surface contours of the land, contours on the water table, under conditions of high and low water tables.

ferent seasons of the year. Figure 4a gives the surface topography of the basin showing the contour lines and the location of six wells. Figure 4b is a profile of the land surface in the plane of the wells numbered 1 to 4. The hillslope is steepest in the middle, gently convex near the hilltop, and slightly concave toward the stream channel at the foot of the hill. The location of the four wells is indicated.

Figure 4d is the same profile, but the depth to the water table is shown as the vertical line beneath each well location. The lower curved line is the profile of the water table. The depth to water is greater near the hilltop than at the foot of the hill. Because the water table emerges at the streambank, the diagram indicates that groundwater is flowing into the stream. This diagram represents conditions during a relatively wet season. As stated earlier, flow in the stream in nonrain periods is sustained by the drainage of stored groundwater. This condition is represented in the diagram.

Figure 4c is the planimetric map of the surface of the saturated zone, the water table. The contours on the surface are equi-potential lines and the spacing of those lines is the gradient of the water surface. This gradient is important because the gravitational force exerted downstream determines the flow velocity for a given frictional resistance, which is a function of the permeability.

Because water flows downhill in the direction of maximum water surface slope, lines drawn orthogonal to these equi-potential contours show the direction of groundwater flow. In the diagram the flow direction is indicated by the arrows.

The conditions described above for a relatively wet season are now contrasted with those for a relatively dry condition in Figure 4f. The ground surface profile is drawn as before, and the wet season profile is drawn in a dashed line. The depth of water shown by the vertical solid line below each well is greater than in the wet season. Again the profile of the water surface is drawn. It has a smaller gradient toward the stream and therefore the flow velocity is smaller than in the previous situation. Figure 4e shows the contours or equi-potential lines on the water table. They are spaced farther apart than in the wet season case. Again the lines drawn perpendicular to these contours indicate the direction of water flow and are shown by arrows.

The simplified diagrams realistically show how field data are used to determine the rate of groundwater flow and the local direction of flow. This simple but true description is valid for an unconfined aquifer and applies to uniform geologic materials only.

Wells and groundwater withdrawal

Underneath much of the dry ground surface there is a groundwater reservoir from which water may be obtained by drilling a well such as those shown in Figure 4.

The discussion thus far seems to indicate that a water table can be found at some depth underground at almost any location. This is indeed true, but more information is needed to predict how much water can be obtained from the underground reservoir. The differences in absorption that exist underground are simulated by the soils in different flower pots. Some seem to require a whole pitcher of water before the bulk of soil becomes saturated to the top. Others might quickly become so full that water seeps out of the drain hole in the bottom before a cupful of water has been applied.

The pore spaces, cracks, and joints between different soils in the different flower pots, and also between different rocks in the earth, vary in amount and number. The amount of water that is poured into the flower pot before it runs out the bottom or overflows is some measure of the pore space available for storing water. If a well is drilled into a particular rock that has a great deal of pore space saturated with water, large amounts of water may be available to the well. But if the rock has only a small amount of pore space, a well may become dry after only a small amount of water is withdrawn. The amount of pore space available is one of two principal factors that determine whether a given rock or soil will be a good source of water for a well. The first factor is called specific yield, meaning the quantity of water that a standard-sized block of such a rock will yield from its cracks and pores.

A rock or soil may have many openings that are filled with water, but if the pores are small or are not connected so that water can flow freely from pore to pore, the rock will not yield all the water it contains. The second factor governing how a rock will act as a source of water is permeability, the quality that determines how readily the pores are able to transmit or allow the water to move. A rock that is a good source of water must contain many pores; it must have a good specific yield, and the pores must be large and connected so the water can flow; it must have high permeability.

Wells that were constructed a century ago were dug wells. Well diggers, with shovel, mattock, and spud, put down a hole one meter or two in diameter and lifted out the dirt by means of a bucket on the end of a rope. When the well was deep enough to reach the water table, or an aquifer, the sides of the hole were strengthened with rock or timbers and the well was complete. Either a pulley was hung over the top or a curb with windlass was built, and buckets were arranged on a rope. When water was needed, the bucket was lowered to the water table, filled, and pulled back up on the rope.

A drilled well is different only in that the hole is put down by means of a bit, which is churned up and down in the hole. Alternatively, a rotary rig is used in which a bit, similar to one used to bore a hole in a piece of wood, is rotated, thus boring itself into the ground. In most modern wells a steel pipe or casing is inserted into the hole, extending the full depth of the well. The casing prevents rocks or dirt that break off the sides of the hole from clogging the opening made by the drilling tool. When the hole has been drilled some distance below the water table, the drilling is stopped and a water pipe is lowered inside the casing. A screen, or well point, which consists of a length of pipe with many perforations that allow water to enter the pipe but exclude sand or dirt is attached to the lower end of pipe. Water is forced up the pipe by means of a motor-driven pump, or a pump driven by a windmill. Most modern wells that supply water for city or irrigation use are equipped with pumps driven by electricity, gasoline, or fuel oil.

Before discussing the pumping of wells, consider an idealized case in Figure 5 of a geologic cross section that has two clay layers that divide a permeable bed of sandstone. The zone above the upper clay layer is permeable throughout and can receive infiltrated water from most parts of the hillslope. Between the two clay layers is a permeable bed that can receive precipitation only in the recharge area. The zone between the impervious layers is a confined aquifer.

Figure 5a shows three wells that extend down to the water table. The casings are perforated to allow water to enter. Water level in each well coincides with the water table that is more more less parallel to the ground surface. At the base of the hill the level of the water in the stream is at the local water table, indicating that the groundwater is contributing to streamflow.

Figure 5b shows three different wells that penetrate the clay layer or aquaclude, the layer of low or zero permeability. These wells are perforated only at their lower end so water enters from the confined aquifer. In the situation shown, the water table in the upper or unconfined aquifer is the same as in 5a, but is different from that of the confined zone. Water rises in the wells to a level that is defined by the pressure within the confined bed. This level is known as the piezometric surface. It decreases slightly in elevation with distance from the local water ta-

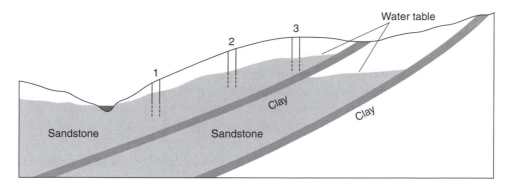

a

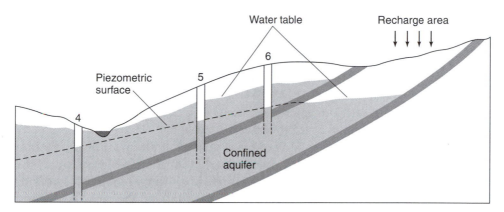

b

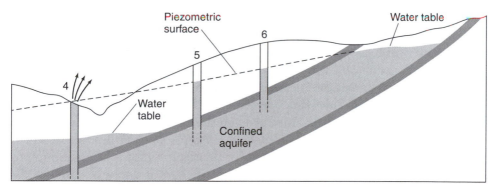

c

Figure 5 Cross sections of a hillslope underlain by sandstone and clay beds. The sandstone is permeable and the clay forms an aquaclude or impervious barrier.

ble in the recharge area. The decrease in elevation results from the frictional resistance to flow in the confined bed.

Figure 5c shows a somewhat different assumed condition in which the water table in the upper unconfined bed is deeper than in 5a and 5b, but the piezometric surface is higher. The slope of the piezometric surface is shown to be the same in 5c and 5b, but is high enough so that it is just above the ground surface at well 4. This well is a flowing artesian well. Wells 5 and 6 are also artesian because the water level in them rises above the aquifer boundary as a result of the natural pressure.

It is interesting to visualize what happens in the vicinity of a well when water is pumped. The pump lifts water out of the hole itself, and thus the water level in the hole is quickly lowered below the general surface of the water table. In the immediate vicinity of the well, water from the pores of the aquifer drains into the hole, lowering the water table near the well. The lowered water table near the well then causes water in pores farther from the well to flow toward the zone near the hole. This occurs on all sides of the well so that the water flows downhill toward the low point in the water table.

If a finger is pressed into a large inflated balloon, causing the taut rubber to stretch smoothly downward from all sides to the tip of the finger, the shape of the depression made by the finger in the balloon surface resembles a cone. This is exactly the shape of the depressed water surface around the well. The pumping of the well creates a "cone of depression" in the water table. The cone is pictured in Figure 6a. Figure 6b shows the same cone as it would look if the unsaturated upper part of the block of ground were lifted up, thus exposing the surface of the water table. Arrows in Figure 6b show how the water moves from all directions toward the center of the cone of depression.

As previously mentioned, the rate of movement of water through a porous material like sand depends on the slope of the water surface. When water is pumped rapidly from the well, the cone of depression is deeper and steeper than when the pumping is slow. Pumping, whatever its rate may be, produces a cone of depression that is steep enough to supply water at the rate of pumping if there is enough water in the ground and if it can move fast enough through the pores of the aquifer.

Replenishment of ground storage

Many miles may separate the place where rain seeps into the earth's surface to become groundwater from the places where that water

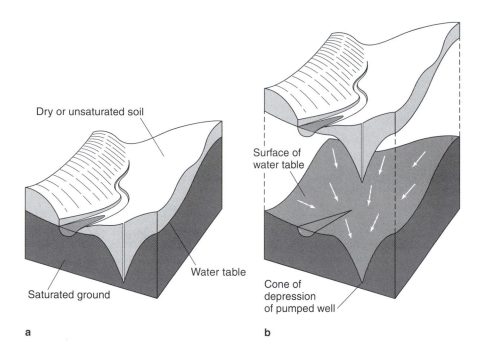

Dry or unsaturated soil

Surface of
water table

Water table

Saturated ground

Cone of
depression
of pumped well

a

b

Figure 6   Effect on the water table of pumping a well. The well causes a drawdown of the saturated zone or a cone of depression.

might reappear. The simple situation discussed earlier showed that water that falls on a hill might enter the ground and flow toward a stream channel nearby and appear as river flow a short distance from the place where it fell as rain. Water also may flow long distances underground before it appears in a surface stream.

There are large areas where the rocks making up the earth's crust occur in distinct layers, and these layers, or strata, differ characteristically in their abilities to transmit water. The earth's crust, as can be seen in many roadside cuts, has been wrinkled, warped, and folded during past geologic ages; rock layers, therefore, seldom lie flat. For this reason it is common for a single bed or layer to be exposed at the surface in one place but extend underground for miles as a sheet. When such a layer is porous, perhaps a layer of sandstone, as shown in Figure 7, it may appear at the surface in one place and be underground at another. Where it is exposed at the surface it may be the area of recharge capable of absorbing rainwater. This is the recharge area of groundwater replenishment.

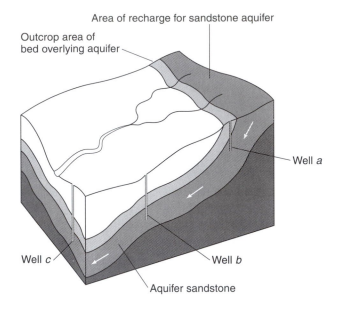

Figure 7   Relation of a recharge area to the aquifer. The waterbearing layer in this diagram dips downward so the wells must be deeper as their distance from the recharge zone increases.

The area of recharge is indicated at the top of Figure 7. Rain falls on this sandy area, sinks into the ground, and flows downhill. Downhill in the area pictured is down the slope of the permeable sandstone bed or layer, as shown by the arrows. The water is flowing toward the lowest position of the water table, just as in the dishpan experiment. In this example, the sandstone layer gets deeper and deeper below the ground surface as it extends away from the recharge point.

Rain falling on an area underlain by rocks that do not readily absorb water moistens the upper soil layers, but the rest of the water flows to the streams and appears as streamflow. Water that wets the soil is returned to the atmosphere by evaporation and transpiration.

The situation pictured in Figure 7 can be found in the Midwest, where the rock strata underlying southern Wisconsin, northern Illinois, and Iowa include some beds composed largely of sandstone. The sandstone is porous, contains large quantities of water, and thus is an aquifer. It is exposed at the surface in a broad belt in south-central Wisconsin. To the east, south, and west of this area, the sandstone beds lie deeper beneath the surface. Many cities and industries obtain their water from wells drilled down into this aquifer.

As in most aquifers, the bulk of the water pumped from these wells fell as rain or snow not more than a few kilometers away. The water percolates downward through the overlying strata, which are not as permeable as the sandstone but which are still capable of transmitting water. Where the overlying beds are of very low permeability, more of the water must come from distant sources, usually 30 or more kilometers away. For example, some of the water pumped from the aquifer at Milwaukee, Wisconsin, fell as rain and snow near Oconomowoc, approximately 40 kilometers west.

How long did it take the water to move that distance? Water moves rather slowly through such rocks under natural conditions—at rates ranging from a few centimeters per year to a meter or more per day. Thus, some of the drops of water pumped from a well at Milwaukee may have taken hundreds of years to travel from near Oconomowoc, but others may have entered the ground nearby and may have taken only months or years to reach the aquifer.

Other extensive aquifers, such as the Madison formation in Wyoming, convey water over great distances. As a rule, however, most aquifers are only of local extent. Many people who own water wells have fanciful notions about the source of water, believing that it "flows in an underground river from the crest of the Appalachian Mountains," or that it taps a "vein of water having its source in northern Canada" or that its source is at the "summit of the Cascade Mountains." Generally they name a cool, wet place of sylvan beauty several hundred kilometers away. There are very few such underground rivers and these are only in limestone regions.

In some areas of the United States, rainfall is so scanty that only occasionally does enough rain fall to add any appreciable amount of water to the groundwater supply. In some of the arid parts of the western United States, water is being pumped that fell as rain during the ice age, at least 10,000 years ago.

Water pumped from a well has been stored underground for months, years, or centuries. Whether a well can be pumped forever depends on whether the water withdrawn from storage is being replaced by new water at an equal rate. The situation may be compared to dipping water out of a bathtub. If the faucet is turned off, continued dipping of the water, cup by cup, will gradually lower the level of the water in the tub. If the faucet is turned on so that there is inflow to compensate for withdrawal, then water may be dipped indefinitely and the level of water will remain approximately the same.

This idea is one of the basic laws of the science of hydrology. When inflow to the storage basin equals outflow or withdrawal, there is no change in the amount of water in storage. When pumpage and natural drainage from an aquifer proceed at a rate equal to the rate at which rain supplies new water, the groundwater level remains the same. If pumping is accelerated, then the water table falls just as does the water level in the tub when the cup removes water faster than the faucet supplies it.

Newspapers have carried many articles about wells going dry during drought years. The wells were being pumped at a rate faster than the rate at which rain was supplying water for replacement. If pumping proceeds too fast for several months or several years, the groundwater level will fall; but if pumping is stopped, sooner or later rainfall will replace the water withdrawn and the water table will return to a level comparable with that existing before pumping began. In arid areas there may not be enough rainfall to contribute recharge in the present climate.

It should be kept in mind that water moves so slowly underground that replenishment by rainfall may take months or years. An average pumping rate that does not exceed the rate of replacement of water by precipitation is desirable. However, determination of the average rate of replenishment is usually difficult. If the amount of water in storage is large, the water level may decrease slowly and a long time may be required to determine whether the aquifer is being overpumped.

Returning to the example of the bathtub, if water is dipped out of the tub with a cup but the amount of water emerging from the faucet is unknown, the only indication of whether the water in storage is being depleted is the level of the water in the tub. If water is to be removed only at the rate of replenishment, the rate of dipping should be adjusted until the level of the water in the tub remains constant over time. A decrease in the water level indicates that dipping has proceeded too rapidly.

If three or four persons, each using a different size cup, dip out of the tub at the same time, while another person turns the handle of the faucet on and off at random, it is obvious that some time will be required to determine whether the rate of removal is greater or less than the rate of replenishment.

A large aquifer is even more difficult to gage. Hundreds of wells may be drawing water from it. The area of recharge may be kilometers away. Rain is heavy one year and light another. Pumping may continue for years before it can be determined that the water supply is large enough to keep all the wells supplied indefinitely. By the time pumping is seen to be excessive, towns have grown and factories and farms have increased their water requirements. No one wishes to give up his well;

so everyone keeps on pumping and the water table gets deeper and deeper.

A fall in the water table is necessary to produce a flow of water to a well. This is the cone of depression around every pumped well. If an aquifer is pumped faster than it is replenished, the water table will continue to fall. Pumps are run by electric or other power, and power costs money. The deeper the water table, and hence the wells, the higher the cost of pumping. If the water table falls, the expense of electricity increases; and if the cost becomes too great, the owner finally finds that he is spending as much for pumping water as he receives for his crops or his product. A well need not go dry to become unusable; a falling water table resulting from several years of deficient rainfall or from over-pumping may result in abandonment of the well because of the increased cost of power.

The groundwater resource

Until the early 1900s, it might have been easy to talk about groundwater in an entirely dispassionate way because all the mechanisms available to draw water to the surface could hardly make a dent in the immense supplies of water. Windmills, animal-driven lifts, and hand pumps could not deliver more than few liters per minute and then only from shallow aquifers whose water table was ten meters or less below the ground surface. People in affluent and humid countries did not appreciate their favorable cicumstance.

I recall being driven by jeep into a small town on the Gangetic plain of north India where, as usual, the town center was crowded with people. As the jeep approached, a happy crowd waved and shouted the equivalent of "Americans!" Then I saw that in the town center was a bright new hand pump, the handle of which was energetically being operated by a young man. From the mouth of the little pump came a gush of clear water, a commodity previously unknown. I learned later that a week earlier, the American AID organization had just completed this simple well to the delight of the populace. Such a homely amenity as a hand pump is not available to millions of people in the third world.

The introduction of motor-driven pumps and the advent of cheap power from electricity or natural gas made groundwater withdrawal a major underpinning of civilization, although one that was not available to many. In the many areas of low rainfall, the exploitation of a limited resource is becoming increasingly menacing. During the glacial period, precipitation was generally higher than it is today and large volumes of water were stored in aquifers. When the world climate became warmer, many regions that became semiarid or arid had extensive quantities of stored water underground that, when extracted, would not be replaced. As their populations increased, these arid regions were the ones most in need of a water supply. The motor-driven pump provided the means of withdrawing this water and as a result, the water table dropped dramatically.

Libya and Saudi Arabia are two countries in which the economy is based on nonrenewable fossil water. Gary Gardner of World Watch described the concrete pipe ordered by Qadhafi to carry water 750 kilometers from the southern desert of Libya to the north coast. The pipe is four meters in diameter, large enough to drive a truck through. This 25 billion dollar project probably will cost the country 10 percent of its oil revenue and will import thousands of laborers into the country, laborers who will be dependent on a resource that will disappear.

Under the Kingdom of Saudi Arabia there is an estimated 2,000 billion cubic meters of water that provide 88 percent of the country's water. According to Gardner, the aquifer supplies 80 percent of the irrigation water and 50 percent of the urban water of the kingdom. Renewable aquifer water, together with desalinated and recycled waste water, meets only about one third of the nation's present water use.

In both Libya and Saudi Arabia, population growth will call for even more draft from the nonrenewable storage volume.

These desert countries are not alone in the overdraft of groundwater. In the High Plains of the United States, a similar scenario has developed in a region that cannot be called a desert. The facts concerning the Ogallala Formation and the history of its development are well known, as is the final outcome. This formation extends from South Dakota to Texas and contains about twice the amount of water stored under Saudi Arabia.

The Ogallala water is used primarily for irrigation and has transformed the former Dust Bowl into a productive agricultural region. The water withdrawn from this aquifer increased enormously between 1949 and 1988. The water level declined more that 4 meters in much of the region and more than 12 meters in isolated places. Gardner reports that by 1980, Kansas had consumed 38 percent of its share of the resource and Texas more than 20 percent. Between 1978 and 1984, the annual cost of pumping reached $7,800 or more on individual farms. One hundred fifty thousand hectares were taken out of production because the cost of pumping was too great.

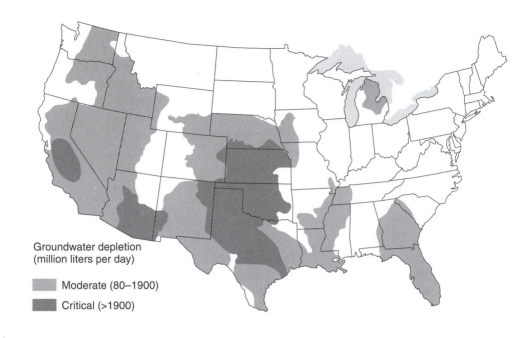

Groundwater depletion
(million liters per day)

Moderate (80–1900)
Critical (>1900)

Figure 8 Extent of groundwater depletion in various parts of the United States. (Adapted from Raven, Berg, and Johnson, *Environment*, Saunders College Publishing, 1995.)

The Phoenix valley and Gila River region of Arizona is another example of serious overdraft of the groundwater resource. Most of the area formerly irrigated has been taken out of production and urbanized because pumped water is too costly to support farming. The extraction of water has resulted in great cracks in the ground as the result of subsidence, an affliction in parts of the central valley of California and which is also very serious in Mexico City.

Figure 8 shows the extent of overdraft in various regions of the United States. However, overdraft is only one of the serious problems in groundwater management. Other problems involve water rights and contamination of underground supplies.

Water rights to ownership of groundwater are complicated by the fact that the laws, even legal doctrines, were developed in the past when the science of water movement and data on water resources and withdrawal were rudimentary. As a result, legal cases, decisions, and concepts are riddled with unscientific and ill-defined terms such as "percolating waters," "subflow," and "overlying rights." Some legal cases discuss the "right of an overlying owner to naturally percolating water." In this concept, water that is part of a stream is not percolating and not subject to an overlying right. A stream is considered to include subsurface flow, whereas percolating water is considerd to come not from a stream or river but rather from uphill sources. The reader can see how the meaning of such statements is confusing.

When terms and concepts are difficult to quantify and are subject to different opinions regarding their meaning, their use leads to litigation and dispute. Even as new knowledge emerges, it is not possible to clear away outmoded words from the lexicon. For this and other reasons, rights to groundwater continue to be a never-ending source of conflict.

An example is the controversy over water in the Safford Valley of the Gila River in Arizona. The Gila River was once a flowing river that supported beavers and trout. Around 1900, saltcedar (Tamarisk sp.) was imported into the watershed by the U.S. Indian Service for stabilization of eroding riverbanks. Saltcedar is notorious as a phreatophyte, a plant that transpires large amounts of water. Studies by the Geological Survey showed that a stand of this species will draw annually from the ground 5 to 9 acre feet per acre (15,000 to 27,000 cubic meters per hectare). Early in the century, these trees stretched for miles in dense stands, drawing heavily on near-surface groundwater. The great floods of the first decades destroyed these stands and before the plants could return in force, farms were developed that were irrigated from a dense network of shallow wells that can be seen in Figure 9. This intensive withdrawal from groundwater resulted in the Gila River becoming dry in some summer months. In an important court case, the water rights of the original Indian tribes were affirmed. Because the tribes had utilized only a portion of the available water within the San Carlos Reservation, the saltcedar has returned and is a dense stand west of the reservation line near Geronimo, in contrast to the irrigated land just upstream.

In 1995, the Indian tribes filed suit to claim water now being used by the upstream farmers. If the court orders the upstream farmers to cease farming, the phreatophytes will return and water utilization (water loss) will increase several-fold. This is merely one example of the controversy surrounding water rights and the confusion that can result.

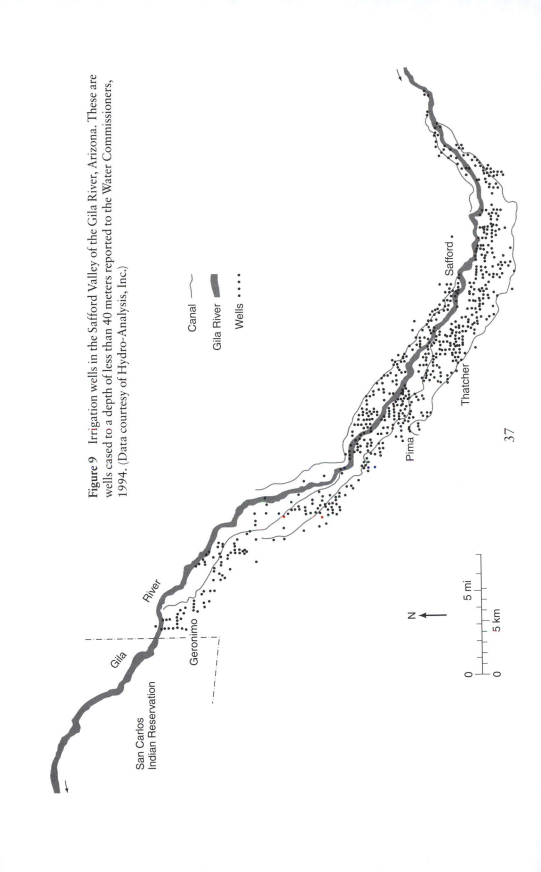

Figure 9 Irrigation wells in the Safford Valley of the Gila River, Arizona. These are wells cased to a depth of less than 40 meters reported to the Water Commissioners, 1994. (Data courtesy of Hydro-Analysis, Inc.)

37

Surface Water

Concepts of surface runoff

Water that is not infiltrated flows downhill over the ground surface. As water moves over the surface, it gradually is collected in rills or small channels, which join to form larger channels, which also join together. The overland flow phase means that water is flowing in a shallow sheet. Water flowing through the grass of a suburban lawn is moving as overland flow. Just as in a bathtub, some depth must be built up before downhill movement begins. Measurements made on natural hillslopes under typical rain conditions show that the depths of water in overland flow near the top of a hill are between 1 and 2 mm. At a distance of 30 meters downhill from the hillcrest, the depth of the water sheet may be 0.5 to 1 cm.

During a heavy rainfall, water can be seen running over the surface of the ground between blades of grass, between the tilled rows in a cultivated field, or even below the leaf and twig layer of the forest floor. On a steep pavement, hard rain often can be seen as a sheet of water flowing downhill. This "sheet flow" is best seen at night, illuminated by a flashlight or the light of passing automobiles. The sheet flow makes a glimmering reflection. Such surface flow runs downhill to the nearest rill, creek, or gutter drain. If the sheet flow is visible, the headwater creeks are certainly carrying storm water down to the bigger creeks and rivers. This is the visible part of the hydrologic or water cycle.

Water drains from the land through streams that increase in size from small hillside rills to majestic rivers that discharge into the oceans. Each rill, brook, creek, or river receives water from an area or tract of land surface that slopes down toward the channel. Channels, therefore, occupy the lowest part of the landscape. The ridges of the land surface—that is, the rims separating the land that drains into one stream from the land that drains into another—are the watershed divides. The area enclosed by the divide is the drainage area or watershed. The most famous divide is the Continental Divide, which separates the streams that flow toward the Pacific Ocean from those that flow toward the Atlantic Ocean or Gulf of Mexico.

The drainage area or drainage basin above any particular point refers to the area bounded by watershed divides from which water drains or flows downhill to or past the point in question.

Rills and headwater extensions of small channels do not extend to the watershed divide. All the precipitation that falls on the unrilled or unchanneled part of a drainage basin but is not infiltrated must flow overland as sheet flow toward the channels or rills. The details of the process of infiltration and overland flow were first explained in the 1930s by the famous engineer, Robert E. Horton. His explanation, called the Horton model, was not only widely accepted but was presumed to be general in its applicability. He stated that surface runoff begins as soon as the rate of precipitation exceeds the rate of infiltration and after certain initial minor losses have been satisfied. If the intensity of rainfall falls below the infiltration rate at any time, surface runoff continues for a short time from the storage represented by the depth of the sheet of flowing water. Another burst of precipitation at an intensity greater than the infiltration rate causes another period of surface runoff. His principal point was that in a small basin, all parts of the drainage area have essentially similar infiltration rates. When this rate of infiltration is exceeded by precipitation intensity, all parts of the basin contribute to surface runoff. An example of Hortonian runoff from a heavy rain in a semi-arid landscape is shown in Figure 10.

Because at any point on an unrilled hillslope, the water moving as overland flow consists of all the water flowing from places uphill or upstream, the depth of flow increases downhill and downstream. In other words, the farther a point is downhill, the larger the contributing drainage area, the greater the depth of flow, and the greater the flow quantity.

Thus the Horton model assumes that at times of intense rainfall, all parts of a small drainage area contribute to surface runoff. Indeed, this can be observed in the semi-arid western United States where vegetal cover is sparse and infiltration is low. But in forested areas where

Figure 10 Overland or sheet flow, typical of Hortonian runoff, during a rainstorm on the Pescado Basin near Ramah, New Mexico.

there is a deep layer of organic litter or duff on the surface, overland or surface flow is not observed, even during the most intense rainfall. All the precipitation apparently is infiltrated; yet the small rills do discharge water. If water generally is not observed to flow overland, how does water reach the headwater tributary rills or channels?

A group of forest hydrologists of the United States Forest Service and the Tennessee Valley Authority developed an alternative to the Horton model. Their model is predicated on the assumption that the area within a drainage basin that contributes water as overland or surface flow changes with time. These hydrologists observed that, depending on conditions, only the part of a basin that was very near the channels contributed to surface runoff; the rest of the basin area, further away, made no contribution. This contributing area expanded and contracted, depending on temporal conditions. Hydrologists therefore called their model the variable source or partial area model and the runoff process is called saturated overland flow. The specific and definitive measurements to prove the validity of this view were furnished by Thomas Dunne of the University of California at Santa Barbara.

According to the partial area model, there are swale bottoms and other areas near the heads of rills and channels that remain relatively moist even between storms. These areas constitute the only part of the total drainage basin that contributes water to the storm hydrograph, the plot of runoff rate as a function of time. When there is a moderate amount of rainfall, the areas near the rill heads quickly become saturated and the infiltration rate approaches zero. All rainfall in such areas runs off immediately because the local soil is saturated. It is common experience to find that swale bottoms at the headwater tips of channels are moist, often even wet, and would infiltrate little or no water if additionally wetted by rain. Such moist zones can often be identified by a color that differs from the dry hillslopes. This is because the local water table is near the surface and capillarity provides water to the near-surface soil. The area of contribution to surface runoff, then, is localized near the upstream tips of the minor channels and rills and along the channel. As rain persists, the percentage of the total basin that contributes to surface runoff increases. The area of contribution can be viewed as a bulb or local zone near the head of every rill that expands and contracts over time.

In an actual field example, Thomas Dunne mapped the area contributing water as direct surface runoff. The small extent of this bulb-shaped area relative to the whole hillside area can be seen in Figure 11. Note that the area of the stream channel itself and its moist edges constitute an important percentage of the total contributing area.

Because a long time is required for subsurface or infiltrated water to move even the short distance to the nearby channel, such water arrives later than the direct runoff and does not contribute to the peak flow. Rather it makes only a modest contribution to the recession limb of the storm hydrograph after the peak has passed and when the flow rate in the channel is decreasing.

The infiltrated water not lost through evaporation or transpiration recharges the stored groundwater, which moves slowly toward the

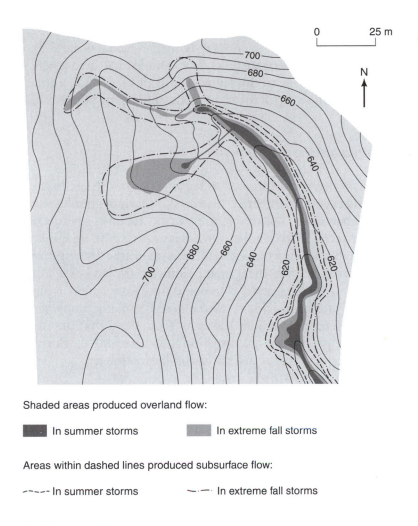

0   25 m

N

Shaded areas produced overland flow:

▮ In summer storms   ▦ In extreme fall storms

Areas within dashed lines produced subsurface flow:

----- In summer storms   —·— In extreme fall storms

Figure 11   Areas contributing to surface runoff under various storm conditions, Happy Valley Basin near Danville, Vermont. (Adapted from Dunne and Black, *Partial-area contributions to storm runoff in a small New England watershed*, Water Resources Research, Vol. 6, 1970.)

channel to sustain the low flow of the stream during nonstorm periods.

The variable source concept, which implies that only part of a drainage area contributes water to a storm hydrograph, explains what had earlier been a mystery. In forested areas and other well-vegetated places, water flowing over the surface is never seen. The answer to the previously posed question now seems clear. Only small parts of a basin, those in swales, draws, and low-lying ground near the channel, experience overland or surface flow. An example of an area where no surface sheet flow is seen in the photographs of Figure 12, a small basin where water is flowing in the channel despite a groundcover of leaves.

Water measurement and water data

The flow of a river is expressed as volume per unit time. In the United States, this is cubic feet per second (cfs). Nearly all published records are in English units, but in scientific work the units are metric, cubic meters per second. To visualize flow, it is necessary to imagine a trough 1 meter high and 1 meter wide, filled with water flowing toward the end of the trough. Each linear meter along the trough holds 1 cubic meter. If 1 cubic meter of water is to be discharged from the trough every second, the speed or velocity of the water moving along the trough must be 1 meter per second. It can be seen, then, that the rate of discharge is the product of cross-sectional area (width times depth) and velocity. The formula for discharge can be written as

$$\text{Discharge} = \text{width} \times \text{depth} \times \text{velocity}$$
$$= \text{area} \times \text{velocity}.$$

Measurement of the rate of discharge or flow of a river thus consists of measuring the cross-sectional area of the flowing water and its mean velocity and then multiplying the two. In practice, the hydrographer uses a current meter, which consists of a propeller that is activated by the flowing water and whose rate of rotation depends on the water velocity. Each time the propeller or vane makes a complete rotation, it closes an electrical circuit that is powered by a pocket battery and makes a click or noise in an earphone. The hydrographer listens to the clicks while watching a hand-held stop watch and recording how many clicks or propeller revolutions are heard during a particular period. Entering the number of propeller revolutions and number of seconds of time in a table, the hydrographer reads the water velocity as meters per second. Newer electronic devices do much of this automatically.

The current meter is placed in the river at a depth where the average or mean velocity is expected. This depth is usually $^6/_{10}$ of the distance from the water surface to the stream bed, inasmuch as the water velocity is large at the surface and decreases to zero at the stream bed. The velocity is clocked in the manner just described for 20 to 30 positions across the river. At each location the local velocity is multiplied by the measured depth and by the width of the zone represented by the par-

Figure 12   A small basin on which saturated overland flow is the process by which runoff occurs. Two photographs show the leaf-covered surface where surface flow is seldom seen, yet where water flows in the stream. (Epping Forest north of London, photos by George Dury.)

ticular velocity and depth. The resulting product is the discharge of that zone. The zone discharges are added to give the discharge of the whole river.

At low flow the current meter measurement may be made by a hydrographer who wades in the river and holds the wading rod, a rigid metal post that is held vertically and along which the meter can be positioned at the desired distance above the stream bed. If the water is too deep for wading, the hydrographer mounts a cable car supported above the river on a steel cable stretched between supports on either side of the channel. The current meter is lowered from the cable car into the river by means of a winch or reel that unwinds a thin wire rope to which the meter is attached. Under the meter and attached to it is a weight or lead fish that keeps the wire rope stretched and holds the meter in a position directly under the cable. The torpedo-shaped lead weight should be 10 to 15 kilograms for rivers of moderate size but should be 25 kilograms or more in big rivers. Many large rivers are measured from a highway bridge rather than from a cable car. To obtain such measurements, the winch is mounted on a wheeled frame that can be braced against the handrail of the bridge when the current meter and weight are to be lowered over the side.

At the time the discharge measurement is made, the elevation of the water surface is recorded. This is read from a simple gage plate or staff gage, an enamel plate attached firmly to a support. The plate is graduated in centimeters. The reading represents the water elevation at the point where the water surface submerges the plate. This reading is called the gage height. The zero reading or gage datum is usually set for convenience; that is, the gage height does not represent the water depth because the zero reading on the gage plate is not necessarily at the stream bed elevation. The elevation of the gage datum (zero reading) above mean sea level is often determined by a leveling survey from a nearby benchmark or known elevation.

A continuous record of water surface elevation is kept on a chart or on a punched tape in the gaging station. Most people have noticed a round corrugated pipe topped with a roof standing on a bridge or a near a river. Inside this structure is a paper-covered drum driven by a clock mechanism. The pen that is drawing an ink record on this chart is activated by a float resting in the water that fills the lower part of the tube or structure. This water comes through a pipe that connects the inside of the gage house to the river, so that wherever the water surface is in the river, the same level is maintained in the gage house. As the river rises or falls, the float inside the gage house rises or falls in unison,

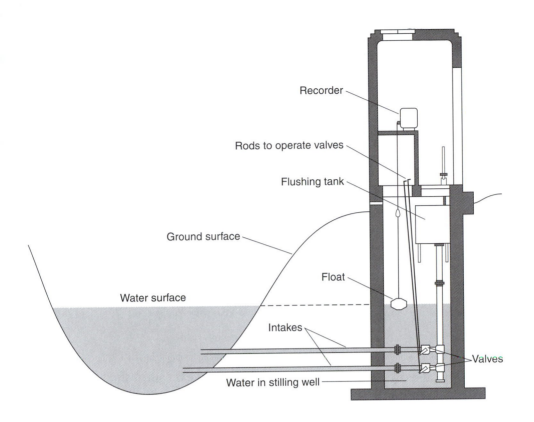

Figure 13 Diagram of a gaging station showing the relation of water in the stilling well to the level in the river.

and thus the recorder provides a graph of water surface elevation as it changes with time. Newer instruments are replacing the paper and pen. Gage height is punched on a paper tape that is later read on computer. Also in use are pressure tranducers that record on a chip that later can be analyzed and plotted by computer.

The gaging station shown in Figure 13 includes the essential features of a typical gage house. The main elements of the station are the intake pipes, which equalize the water surface elevation in channel and in gage house, and the float, which is connected to a recorder.

The gaging station provides a record of water surface elevation. This record must be translated into flow rate, which in turn, can be used to compute volume of water. The current meter observations provide the necessary link. By plotting the computed discharge at the time of a current meter measurement against the concurrent gage height

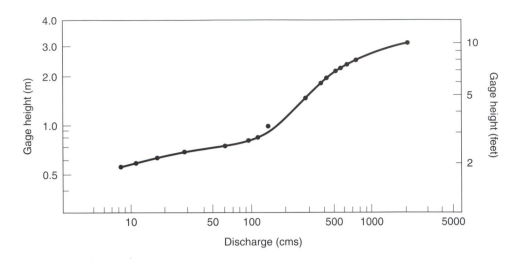

Figure 14 Rating curve for Seneca Creek near Dawsonville, Maryland.

(staff gage reading), one point of a rating curve is established. The rating curve, or relation of gage height to discharge, is an empirical relation derived from the current meter observations.

Selected pairs of values of discharge and gage height are also published for the highest peak discharges during each year of record. Often these values do not represent current meter measurements during the flood; rather, they are recorded gage heights taken from continuous record at the gage. The corresponding discharge is read from a previously established rating curve.

The discharge and gage height values for the gaging station for a given year are plotted on double logarithmic paper and result in a rating curve similar to that shown in Figure 14. When enough current meter observations are available to establish the relationship typified by Figure 14, it is possible to interpolate, that is, to read the discharge for any given gage height. The gage height is read at various hours of the day from the pen trace or tape; these figures are then entered into the rating curve and the discharge is read. The discharges may then be averaged to obtain the average flow for the day. This figure is tabulated for each day of the year and, together with certain other data, is included in a series published by the United States Geological Survey titled, for example, *Water Resources Data for Maryland and Delaware, Part 1, Surface Water Records*. Each state (or, in the case of small states, each pair of states) is represented each year in this series that has been published since 1961.

To reduce the volume of material to be held permanently on library shelves, five-year summaries are published in a more permanent form: the *Water Supply Papers of the United States Geological Survey*. The summaries have daily discharge values for each of the five years included. These summaries may be found in most large libraries along with other scientific reports of the United States Geological Survey. Each such volume holds all the water supply papers containing similar data for the same geographic area for various years. For some states, some of these data are also available on CD-ROM.

The hydrograph

The flow of a river is variable through time because the precipitation that feeds the river is variable. During a storm, water is contributed by rivulets to small creeks and thence to larger rivers; when the storm is over, the water drains away and discharge rates return to normal. The hydrologist is concerned with the time variation of flow.

A plot of discharge or flow rate as a function of time is the hydrograph. Time may be shown in minutes, hours, days, or other units, and discharge generally is shown in cubic meters per second (cms), or cubic feet per second (cfs). Figure 15 is a typical hydrograph showing a rather simple storm peak. The values plotted are the average flow for each day

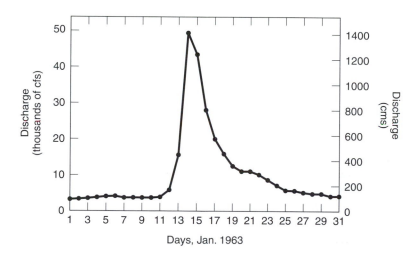

Figure 15 Hydrograph showing plot of discharge as a function of time for the Potomac River near Washington D.C. for January, 1963.

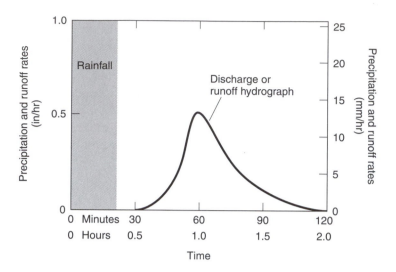

Figure 16 Typical hyetograph showing rainfall rate as a function of time and the resulting hydrograph.

one year in January in the Potomac River near Washington D.C. The drainage area above that gage is 29,940 square kilometers.

The relation of precipitation during a storm to the consequent hydrograph of a river is simpler for small basins than for large ones, primarily because rainfall over any large area is not uniform in time or space. A typical relationship between rainfall over a small area (a few hectares up to a square kilometer) and time, the hyetograph, is diagrammed in Figure 16. For illustrative purposes, the ordinate of the graph is shown in millimeters per hour over the catchment area or drainage basin. This unit applies equally well to rainfall and to discharge in the stream. To convert the discharge to the usual English units or cubic feet per second (cfs), the following approximation is useful: 1 inch/hour from one acre = 1 cfs.

The figure might realistically represent a rainstorm on an area of 2.6 square kilometers. The rainfall lasted 20 minutes (1/3 hour) and its average intensity was 2.5 cm per hour (1 inch per hour). Ordinarily, this would be considered a short but intense rain: 0.84 cm (0.33 inches) of rain fell. The amount of rain is the product of intensity and time. Because the ordinate scale is a rate and the abscissa scale is time, the area under a graph such as a hyetograph is a volume. So the gray area in Figure 16 is the volume of rain.

By the same reasoning, the area under a hydrograph is the volume of runoff. Because the volume of rain is much larger than the volume of runoff, the ordinate scales for rainfall and runoff are different. Inspection of the hydrograph shows that runoff at the place of measurement did not begin until some 5 minutes after the rainfall had ceased. All the runoff had passed downstream within 2 hours after the storm began.

If the area to which Figure 16 applies is 2.6 square kilometers, then the peak rate of flow shown on the hydrograph is 9.3 cubic meters per second.

Figure 16 shows that the peak flow at the place where the basin area is 2.6 square kilometers occurred one hour after the beginning of the rain. This is the correct order of magnitude of time for a basin of such size. The figure also shows that the center of mass of the hydrograph lags or follows the center of mass of the rainfall by approximately one hour. Again, this is consistent for a basin of this size.

The storm hydrograph typically has the shape shown in Figure 16. The part of the flow preceding the peak is called the rising limb; the part following the peak is called the recession limb. The peak or peak flow refers to the moment of highest discharge in the storm period.

Channel storage

In a flow system, whether it be the bathtub, the garden hose, or a river, some water must accumulate temporarily in the system before the incoming water flows out at the other end. When a person waters the garden, he turns on the faucet but the water does not immediately flow out of the other end of the hose unless the hose is already full of water. There will be a short period during which the hose becomes full before any water is discharged at the lower end. Similarly, if the faucet is turned off, the water that is in the hose drains out; therefore, the outflow does not stop at the same moment that the inflow ceases.

The amount of water in the hose could be thought of as being stored temporarily in the flow system. So it is with rivers. When tributaries contribute flow to the upper end of a river channel, a certain amount of time is required for that water to appear at the lower end. After the tributary inflow stops, the water that is in transit in the river channel gradually drains out. Therefore, the water in transit, or the channel storage, is comparable to a reservoir, or the bathtub. Enormous volumes of water are present in the channels during major floods. For example, during the flood of the Ohio River in January

1937, the volume of storage in the channel system was computed by Hoyt and Langbein to be 69 cubic kilometers (56,000,000 ac. ft.), a volume greater than the capacity of a large reservoir.

Because the river channel system is a form of temporary storage, it tends to reduce the height of the flood. As a flood moves down the river system, the temporary storage in the channel reduces the flood peak. The situation is the same as when the faucet is turned on full tilt for a short time but the drain discharges water at a somewhat lower rate because of the temporary storage of water in the tub or sink itself. Storage tends to make the maximum rate of outflow less than the maximum rate of inflow.

The effect of channel storage can be seen in the discharge hydrograph. The typical shape of a hydrograph was illustrated in Figure 16. The falling or recession limb has a point of inflection between the convex early part and the concave later part. This point of inflection represents the time when runoff into the upstream channel has ceased. All the flow after the point of inflection is water that accumulated as channel storage and is now draining out. The relation among inflow, outflow, and storage in a reach of river channel is complicated by the fact that on the rise of the hydrograph, a considerable amount of water usually infiltrates into the channel banks and later drains back into the channel as the flow recedes.

The storage equation

Flow over a surface or in a channel cannot begin until an appreciable depth is attained because the speed or velocity depends on depth as well as gradient and roughness. For example, a bathtub faucet represents the source of inflow and the drain represents the outlet. When the faucet is turned on, water usually does not immediately flow out the drain at a rate equal to the inflow because the drain outlet must be covered with water. If the faucet is opened one-quarter turn, allowing enough water for a person to wash his hands, and if the drain outlet is fully opened, water accumulates in the tub even though some is constantly draining away. As the depth of water in the tub increases, the rate of outflow increases until finally the outflow rate equals the inflow. The depth of water in the tub gradually becomes stabilized when outflow rate equals inflow from the faucet. This situation will persist almost indefinitely. When the faucet is closed, inflow ceases. If the depth of the water in the tub is several centimeters, the water will drain out at a gradually decreasing rate as depth decreases.

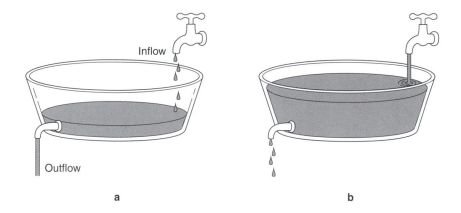

Figure 17 Relation of storage to inflow and outflow: a, inflow less than outflow; b, inflow greater than outflow.

The action of water flowing in and out of the bathtub exemplifies the storage equation, which states:

Rate of outflow = rate of inflow ± change of storage.

In other words, if inflow equals outflow, the amount of water in storage is constant. When inflow exceeds outflow, the amount of water in storage is increasing. If the flow of water into the bathtub just described is zero, then the outflow comes only from the stored water and storage decreases at a rate that is directly dependent on outflow. Inflow and outflow are exemplified in Figure 17.

The principle of the storage equation operates in surface runoff and in channels. It also applies to reservoirs designed to hold water during periods of high flow (inflow exceeds outflow and storage increases). At times of low inflow, the stored water is released (outflow exceeds inflow by releasing stored water). In flood control reservoirs, high inflow is stored, to be released later at acceptable outflow rates.

In a drainage basin, tributaries successively join and the main channel becomes larger farther downstream. Each tributary has a hydrograph describing the relation of discharge to time during a storm event. When a tributary meets or enters another channel, the waters of the two are added but the peaks of their respective hydrographs do not necessarily coincide. One channel may have passed its peak and be in the recession limb at the time the joining channel is still on the rising side of its hydrograph. The lack of simultaneity of peaks at the joining point results in a lower peak than would occur if the peaks arrived simultaneously.

An example might help to clarify this statement. Assume that a basin of 155 square kilometers (60 square miles) has three main tributaries, the junctions of which are equal distances apart, as shown in Figure 18a. Let each of the three subbasins or each of the three tributaries drain 26 square kilometers (10 square miles). The remainder of the whole basin drains into smaller channels that feed directly to the main stream. The three main subbasins thus total 78 square kilometers (30 square miles) or half the area of the main basin at D.

Assume also that during a rainstorm, 25 mm or 1 inch of precipitation was made available for runoff in 4 hours. A larger amount of rain fell during the storm, but the present computation is concerned mainly with "precipitation excess," or that part of the precipitation appearing as runoff in the storm hydrograph. This is the gray area in Figure 18b.

The hydrograph labeled I in Figure 18b is computed to be the flow at the mouth of the subbasin at A. This water must flow down the channel from A to D, which takes a certain amount of time. During its travel from A to D it must successively fill the channel and then drain away downstream. The volume of water in the channel in the reach between A and D acts in the same manner as the water in the bathtub or the water in a storage reservoir. The computation of inflow, outflow, and storage for a reach of river is called flood routing. Hydrograph I has been routed through successive reaches of channel; the effect of the channel storage can be seen on the routed hydrographs. The first routing represents the change in a routing distance of 2 hours and produced the hydrograph II. That is, for this computation, hydrograph I was considered the inflow graph and II was the computed outflow after traveling downstream a distance equivalent to 2 hours. Hydrographs III and IV were the results of routing 6 hours and 9 hours, respectively.

It can be seen that channel storage, acting as a bathtub or reservoir, decreases the flood peak as the hydrograph moves progressively downstream. The original hydrograph peak at A was 28 cms and occurred approximately 5 hours after the beginning of precipitation. By the time the flood wave reached 12.8 kilometers downstream, the peak was only 17 cms, and it occurred 13 hours after the beginning of precipitation.

If the storm had covered all of the 155 square kilometer basin, the hydrographs for each of the three subbasins would have been the same. But because the subbasins are at different distances above D, the water from the nearest one entering at C would already have drained partly away by the time the contribution from the farther ones, B and A, arrived at D.

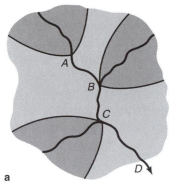

Figure 18 Basin map and hydrographs of subbasins in a drainage area of 155 sq km (60 sq mi) having three subbasins of 26 sq km (10 sq mi) each. The runoff of each of the subbasins is routed downchannel in 18b. The addition of the discharges of these is added to give the discharge of the whole basin in 18c. (Adapted from Leopold and Maddock, *The Flood Control Controversy*, Ronald Press, 1954.)

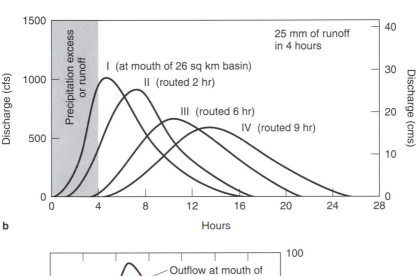

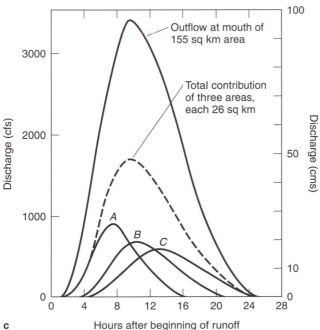

55

This difference in distance determines both the timing and peak of flow at the time the hydrographs of various tributaries pass a downstream point. Figure 18c shows the contributions from subbasins *C*, *B* and *A* at point *D*. The hydrograph from *A*, having been routed the farthest, is later and has a lower peak than the hydrographs from *B* or *C*.

When the three hydrographs are added at point *D*, the sum is the dashed graph. Because *A*, *B*, and *C* are only half of the area upstream of point *D*, and the remaining half is assumed to have a similar contribution, the computed hydrograph of the 155 square kilometers has been shown as the largest solid line graph in Figure 18c. It represents twice or double the dashed-line graph from the three contributing subbasins.

The downstream hydrograph is thus built from the addition of contributions from upstream areas, each routed or altered as a result of the storage in the channel through which it flows.

The velocity of water in channels

The saying that still water runs deep may be a good statement to apply to human nature, but it is not good hydrology. Still waters may be shallow or deep, and the deep waters may run slowly or fast.

When a river rises, the water moves faster. For example, when the river is low during a dry spell, the water may be moving at an average rate of approximately 12 centimeters per second, or approximately 0.43 kilometers per hour. When the river is in flood, its current may be as much as 2 meters per second. At a measuring section of the Potomac River in Chain Bridge gorge near Washington, D.C., during the flood of March 1936, the speed of the water was 6.7 meters per second, about the highest velocity measured in natural river channels with a current meter by the United States Geological Survey.

At any place, then, as water becomes deeper it tends to flow faster. When it moves downhill, water acts like any other body that is moved by gravity. It would move ever faster, like a ball rolling downhill, were it not held in check by friction against the channel bed and banks. The speed at which water moves is a balance between gravity and friction. But as the water in any natural stream gets deeper, the area against which the water rubs does not substantially increase. For this reason, gravity becomes more important to water velocity as the river deepens.

How does the water speed change along its course from a river's mountainous source to its mouth? In the upstream part, the mountain brooks appear to rush downhill as a thrust of turbulent white water. They appear to exhibit a high-velocity flow. On the other hand, the large river near the mouth seems to sweep majestically around its bends in a stately, slow motion. But appearances can be deceiving. It is better to rely on a current meter to determine water-flow velocity.

The current meter shows that the water in the mountain stream on a clear day may be tumbling along at an average rate of approximately 0.4 meters per second. The current in the big river far downstream may be 1.0 to 1.5 meters per second at low flow, and all the creeks and tributaries in between move along at intermediate speeds. Water speed increases farther downstream. The difference between appearances and current meter readings is merely a matter of interpretation. Again, the connecting link is depth. At points further downstream, there is more water, and both depth and width of the river increase. Therefore, to call a mountain stream a torrent implies that it is flowing rapidly in relation to its shallow depth. To say that a big river is sluggish implies that the water is moving slowly relative to its great depth.

In periods of flood, small streams in headwater areas have average water velocities of 1.5 to 2.5 meters per second; large rivers, such as the Mississippi, have average water velocities of 2 to 3 meters per second. There is much variation but these are the measured orders of magnitude.

The velocity of water moving downstream influences the tendency for subbasins entering as tributaries along the river to contribute their share to the main channel at different times. The importance of this staggered contribution in reducing flood peaks is emphasized in the later discussion of the joining of tributaries.

The River Channel—
Formation and Maintenance

The sediment load

The movement of water from precipitation to flow has been discussed. The channel that carries the runoff is that aspect of the river and the creek most obvious to the observer. Its function, formation, and maintenance constitute the crux of the subject of fluvial geomorphology. The channel is carved by the flowing water but it takes the form dictated by the sediment carried. The sediment is ultimately derived from the rocks and soils making up the landmass.

When it rains or when snow thaws, the water in a river becomes muddy because it is carrying sediment that it has accumulated on its way over the land and through the stream channels. Not only is sediment entrained but the mineral material is also dissolved from the rocks and transported as if it were sugar in tea. Water in nature is nearly everywhere in contact with the soil, but the amount of sediment and the dissolved load depend on the geology, the soil forming processes, the vegetation, and the climatic regime. When water is to be used for city supply or for industrial use, sediment in the water is undesirable. It must be removed and then disposed of.

When a reservoir is constructed by damming a river, the sediment load of the river deposits in the still water of the lake. Over time, sediment may fill a reservoir, using up the storage space intended for flood control, irrigation, power, or municipal water supply. Whenever water is handled, sediment is also handled.

Though sediment in rivers often seems a costly nuisance when water is utilized, the river channel is accustomed to carrying sediment as well as water. It is an important characteristic of a natural channel to accept both high and low flows with their associated sediment load without longterm changes in morphology. Indeed, for a channel to maintain its dynamic equilibrium, that is to maintain its morphologic form over many years without appreciable aggradation or degradation, the variety of flows experienced in nature is necessary.

In an individual curve of the channel, the concave bank tends to erode and the convex bank advances, keeping the channel width about the same. It is the sediment load, not the water, that keeps the channel shape constant. Channel shape, size, and properties are altered by the processes of erosion and deposition of sediment.

When human activities change the sediment load of streams, the channel adjusts itself to accommodate the change just as a human body adjusts to seasonal changes in weather, to new bacteria, to new diet. When a person moves to a different altitude or climate, or changes the dietary environment, subtle changes in metabolic rate or water loss occur. The river similarly adjusts to changes in sediment load or water discharge. Before the nature of these adjustments and their reasons are discussed, some of the native properties of sediment and the action of sediment in water will be considered.

The sediment carried in streams varies in size of particle, shape (round, oblong, and angular), and mineral composition. The most common mineral in river sediment is quartz, the same material that constitutes both common sand and table glassware.

An important characteristic of a sediment is the size of the grains. Most of the words used to describe different sediments are familiar and are used in everyday mention of earth materials. Coarse sediments are usually called gravel. Finer sediments are described as sand, silt, and clay. The smaller the particle, the greater is the surface of the grain relative to its weight. A 2 cm pebble has a surface area of approximately 12 square centimeters. If a 2 cm pebble is broken into particles of clay size, each about 0.0004 cm, the total surface area of the particles is 30,000 square centimeters. The surface area of a grain determines many of its physical properties, such as rate of settling and chemical activity.

If a liter bottle or large jar is filled with water and a handful of soil is added, the water immediately becomes muddy. If the bottle is shaken vigorously and set down, the soil particles begin to settle. The large particles settle to the bottom first; the very fine particles settle slowly and may remain in suspension for a long time. Several hours or days may be required for the water to clear. The accumulation of soil at the bottom of the jar varies from coarse particles at the bottom to fine at the top. The rate at which particles settle in water is determined by their size and weight.

In the jar the process of settling took place while the water was still. However, in a moving stream the motion of flow constantly stirs up the water; and the particles of sediment may be carried along by the water rather than settle out. The river water is being shaken up continuously just as though the bottle were shaken continuously. If the bottle were shaken gingerly and not too rapidly, the fine particles would be kept in suspension and the coarse ones would settle to the bottom.

Turbulent swirls in a big river can keep large particles in suspension. As travel down the river system breaks the rocks into smaller bits, into sand and finally silt, the channel is adjusted in width, depth, and slope to handle the sediment that is received from the upstream river system. The increases in river width and depth downstream are caused by the increasing amount of water as the river gets larger and also by the changes in amount and size of sediment.

In the case of mountain torrents, the slope of the channel is determined by the general topography. Large rocks or boulders simply remain in place until weathering breaks them down to a size that can be transported by the flow, or until a debris flow moves them down the mountain. These steep mountain streams, tumbling over large cobbles and boulders, may remain stable for years or decades until a very large storm delivers sufficient water to cause a channel-scouring flood to occur. Such channels are not true alluvial channels and the relations among the hydraulic and sediment factors do not agree closely with the quasi-equilibrium conditions existing in the rivers and creeks that are the principal examples presented here.

The sediment or rock debris carried by streams is derived from the weathering of rocks on the land. In the headwater areas of mountains, even large rocks can be moved downhill by the combined action of slow creep and moving water. The longitudinal profile of a river is steep in its headwaters, less steep in the middle course, and of gentle gradient still further downstream. This decreasing gradient is related in a general but complex way to the changing discharge and to the changing size of the sediment load.

The mode by which large and small rock particles are carried by running water also differs, although again, size is not the only determinant. Generally, the larger particles move as bedload and the small ones move as suspended load. Bedload is that portion of the moving grain load whose immersed weight is carried by intermittent contact with the immobile bed. The weight of bed grains can be compared to that of a tennis ball that is dribbled or successively bounced off the floor. The floor must ultimately carry the weight of the ball even though the contact between the two is intermittent. Bedload includes the particles that roll, jump, skip, or saltate in an interrupted motion near the bed, never rising very far off the bed.

Suspended load is that part of the moving load whose weight is carried by the column of water in which it is immersed and is supported by the water within the interstices of the bed grains. The turbulence in the flowing water of the channel keeps swirling the suspended grains upward in successive eddies. Between these intermittent upward lifts the suspended grains fall by gravity through the water at a rate dependent on their size.

The suspended load, then, is like a fleet of airplanes that are supported on the column of air. Sailplanes are supported by the updrafts just as suspended particles are kept up in a river by the similar turbulent eddies. In most rivers the load in motion is carried less as bedload than as suspended load. The percentage of the total load in motion carried as bedload is generally in the range of 1 to 6 percent, but it may be in the order of 20 to 50 percent in some rivers under some circumstances. The number of sites on rivers and creeks where simultaneous measurements of bedload and suspended load are made is still very limited so generalizations are tentative. M. Church cites measurements on the cobble-gravel Fraser River in British Columbia in which 18 million metric tons per year comprise only 200,000 tons of bedload, or only 1 percent. Detailed measurements were made by the U.S. Forest Service in 1989 on nine streams in the Front Range of Colorado, a data set known as the Fluvial Sites. Though none of the streams reached bankfull during that runoff season, the bedload yield in all sites was nearly equal to the suspended load yield. As one example, on Left Hand Creek at 2.86 cms, the bedload transport rate and the suspended load rate were both equal to 10 tons per day.

The bankfull stage is when the water fills the channel to the level of the floodplain (features are discussed in detail on later pages). The importance of the bankfull stage becomes clear when the sediment load is considered. Bedload deposition is the process by which the point bar is built and thus is the principal source of material making up the floodplain. But bedload does not move during the many days each year when a river is at low flow. Bedload movement begins at discharges just less than bankfull and the bulk of bedload movement occurs at flows ranging from 90 percent of bankfull to twice bankfull discharge. Some suspended load is carried even by relatively low flows.

The load carried by rivers varies greatly from stream to stream. It is affected by the amount of rainfall, differences in kinds of rock, infiltration capacity of the soil, vegetative cover, and the interaction among them. Watersheds composed of fine windblown soil, as in western Iowa, put a large amount of sediment in the channel during every rainstorm and yield as much as 2,000 tons per each square kilometer per year. Streams draining hard rocks, such as those in the Adirondack Mountains of New York State, carry very little sediment, usually less than 100 tons per square kilometer per year. Finally, plant cover on the land governs sediment yield. Barren areas produce much more sediment than tree-covered ones.

Measurement data show that the sediment in rivers usually varies from about 2 tons per square kilometer per year to about 250 tons per square kilometer per year, with some basins yielding more and some less. The watersheds in the United States contributing the largest amount of sediment are those in the plateau regions of the semi-arid western states; intermediate values are in the sub-humid eastern states, and the lowest values are in the high country of the Rocky Mountains and Adirondacks.

The rate of erosion of soil or rock debris from land does not necessarily equal the load carried by a river downstream. The erosion rate is considerably greater than the downstream transport rate because there are many intermediate zones where sediment is deposited or stored. For very small plots or fields near a watershed divide, such as areas of 2 hectares, perhaps 25 percent of the eroded material can be measured as sediment load in the river. For still larger basins, the percentage decreases. Eroded material is dropped on large areas of floodplains and at the bases of hillslopes, so rivers do not carry away to the ocean more than a small portion of what is annually eroded from the drainage basin surface. Through geologic time, however, a continent is ultimately eroded and dissolved, its surface becoming lower, as the transport processes carry the materials to the ocean.

When a dam is built across a river and sediment settles in the still water of the reservoir, clear water is released to the channel downstream. Because the channel was accustomed to water containing sediment, the clear water causes the channel to change its shape and slope. These changes in channels downstream of dams cannot yet be accurately predicted because of lack of knowledge; nonetheless, we know the changes are causing considerable difficulty to engineering works such as dams, barriers, and bridge piers.

The sources of sediment might at first glance appear to be primarily in the gaping wounds on the landscape in the form of gullies and arroyos. The few data available on sediment budget show that this source is less important than the sheet erosion of sheetwash, rills, and rain splash. Sheet erosion is the most ubiquitous process contributing sediment to most rivers. But in steep forested landscapes, as in the Pacific Northwest of the United States, gully erosion and landslides into gullies are much more important than surface erosion. The erosion in forests where lumbering is an important aspect of human activity, road surfaces and unvegetated sidecast or cut slopes are principal sources of surface eroded material.

The erosion of the concave banks of river curves appears to be an important source of sediment, but material eroded on one bank is usually deposited a short distance downstream. Material eroded from one concave bank tends to be deposited on the same side of the river on the next point bar downstream.

Channel configuration and pattern

The previous discussion concerned the water flowing downstream, its source, measurement, some aspects of its variability, and the changes that occur as it moves down the system. The stream channel carrying this flow experiences short periods of large flow values and much longer periods of little flow. It is somewhat surprising that the channel can accommodate these different conditions without being torn apart by the high discharge or blocked by deposition of sediment. In fact, when unimpaired by humans, the natural condition is nicely balanced and referred to as quasi-equilibrium, in which the size and form of the channel is maintained by the flow of water and sediment with only slow and gradual change. As mentioned previously, the variation in flow is one of the requirements for the maintenance of the channel.

The shape and size that is formed and maintained by the flowing water is not large enough to carry unusually high discharge. Nearly all stream channels, whether large or small, will contain without overflow approximately that discharge that occurs about once a year. Higher flows, occurring on the average only once in 2 years, or once in 5 years or more, will be too large to be contained in the natural channel and will overflow the floodplain, the area adjacent to the stream or river. It is called floodplain because it is part of the river even though it is used only infrequently. In ordinary parlance, a flood is defined as water flowing out of the channel. Where humans use the floodplain they should expect to get wet at times, and flood damage is due to encroachment on a part of the river. The size, shape, and characteristics of the natural channel and its floodplain are the focus of a part of physical geography.

The stream channel in cross section is somewhat rectangular, the width being several to many times the depth. But the section is seldom symmetrical for it is usually deeper near one bank than near the other. If there are curves in the channel, the deep part is near the concave bank and the water gets progressively shallower toward the convex bank. This shallowing is over the point bar, a depositional feature shown in Figure 19a. Even in nearly straight reaches, point bars occur alternately on either side of the channel. This process is exhibited in its most perfect though extreme form in the confined channel of the Colorado River near Needles, California, shown in Figure 20. The flow is controlled by dams upstream and the channel gets its inflow of sediment only from the ephemeral washes that enter the river below the dams. The channel was straightened and reveted with rock for a long distance in the vicinity shown in the photograph. The sand is arranged by the flow in alternate bars symetrically developed at a repeating distance of 3.3 channel widths, somewhat closer together than the bars ordinarily seen in natural channels. Usually, the spacing of alternate bars is 5 to 7 channel widths.

The process leading to the formation of point bars and the floodplain is discussed in the next section.

The alternation of point bars along the channel is related to the alternation of deeps and shallows as shown in Figure 19c. The deep zones or pools alternate with the shallow zone or riffles and together comprise the pool-riffle sequence, which is typical of most channels having beds of mixed gravel, sand, or cobbles. The riffle is a protuberance on the bed, a topographic high.

The diagrams in Figure 19 present several aspects of the channel, point bar, and pool-riffle sequence. Figure 19b shows a typical sinuous channel in which the meander bends have a modest amplitude, with point bars on each convex bank. The diagram presents the main items in the nomenclature including the wave length, radius of curvature, and position of the shallow portion at the crossover or point of inflection of the bend. Figure 19c is a profile through such a reach of channel

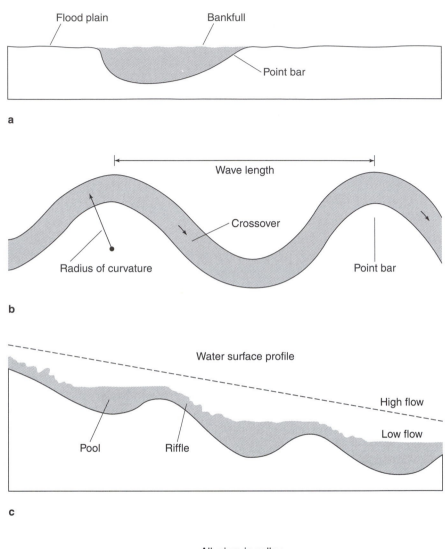

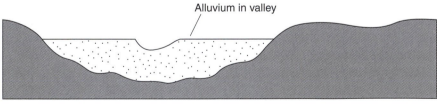

Figure 19 Typical pattern and profile of a sinuous channel with some definitions of features. The cross section in 19a is typical of a channel bend, and 19d shows the relation of the channel to the alluvial deposit and the valley.

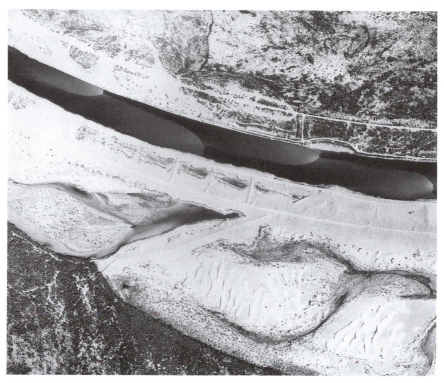

Figure 20 The confined channel of the Colorado River near Needles, California. The sand being carried by the water is arranged by the flow in alternating bars of great symmetry.

indicating that the pool or deep is at the curve and the shallow or riffle is at the crossover. The profiles of water surface at low flow and high flow are also shown.

Figure 19a is a cross section of the channel near bankfull stage, with the floodplain and point bar shown. Figure 19d is the cross section across the valley indicating that the channel is formed in the alluvial or river-laid material that overlies the bedrock. These diagrams are typical of many river valleys and many channels.

In nearly all natural channels the alternation of pools and riffles exists. Only in ephemeral streams, the bed of which is sand, is the topographic undulation not observed and even in those channels, whatever fine gravel is present tends to be distributed in patterns that resemble the usual pool-riffle organization.

In high mountain streams having very steep gradients, deeps and shallows exist of even more pronounced relief, leading to the name of the step-pool sequence. In such a profile the steps corresponding to riffles can even be small waterfalls and the lengths between steps are much shorter than in the usual mixed gravel stream.

This tendency for a symetrically repeating configuration of the profile (Figure 19c) is a highly essential part of the quasi-equilibrium condition because these undulations of the bed constitute an important part of the channel roughness needed to control the velocity of flow. It is known that when such undulations are removed, as in many of the channels that have been dredged or straightened, velocity may become extreme and lead to serious erosion.

Considering the ubiquity of this phenomenon, there have been few serious attempts to explain it. The hypothesis that appears to be unchallenged uses the well-known fact that the interaction between objects moving in a path, as automobiles move on a highway, leads to a bunching up in groups called platoons. In automobile use, all drivers know that the closer cars are together the more slowly they go. Because of the interaction of the cars due to our braking habits, cars bunch up and the platoons of cars are separated by long stretches of open road.

In a similar manner, rocks moved by water in a river interact with one another so that the closer the rocks are together, the more force or stress is needed to move them. This, then, results in rocks congregating in groups, or riffles. In the riffle the rocks are close together or concentrated much as cars close together are concentrated. The pools are the counterpart of the open stretches of road where there are few cars.

This principle explains the concentration of rocks in the riffle but does not explain why the spacing along the river should be uniform, that is why the riffles should be spaced at an average distance apart of from 5 to 7 channel widths.

Rivers, streams, and creeks have many appearances. Some rivers are so wide that they look like lakes. Many channels seem to be rushing torrents, some have the forms of graceful curves and slow motion, and others are dry sandy-looking washes. All of these characteristic forms are natural and logical, stemming from the geology, topography, and vegetative type of the point of origin.

There are different ways of classifying channels, depending on the purpose of the description. Each has merits but for present purposes let us consider only five types, and recognize that all types, however defined, tend to merge or overlap into other types. Also, a given type may characterize only a short reach of channel. With that explanation I will illustrate these types by photographic examples.

By far the most common pattern is the meandering type. I did not appreciate the ubiquity of this pattern type until I mapped channel

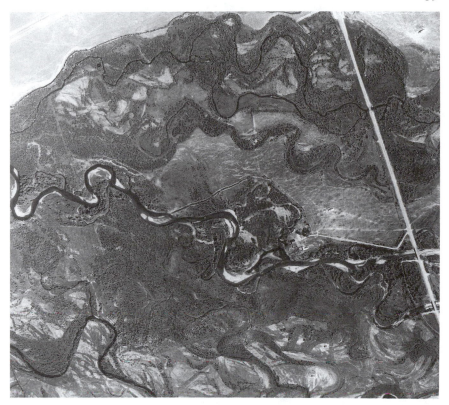

Figure 21 The meandering pattern of the Green River near Daniel, Wyoming. At some time in the past, the river has been at every position across the valley as shown by the remnants of its former locations. A tributary, Horse Creek, is nearly parallel to the Green, and joins the main stream a few kilometers downstream.

types from a light plane over some 5,000 kilometers of river valley and several western states. About 90 percent of the valley distance contained meandering channels while the other stream types were of minor importance.

It must be understood that river channels are curved, sinuous, or meandering because that is the natural and most probable form. It is the form that conserves energy and tends at the same time to make energy expenditure along the streamline most uniform. The physical forces act to promote a curvilinear form. A reach of stream that is straight tends to become curved, and in no known instance does a curved form become straight through any appreciable distance.

Figure 21 shows the meandering channels of various sizes developed on the floodplain of the Green River near Daniel, Wyoming. The

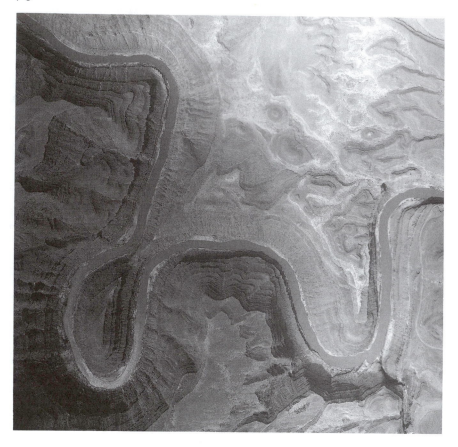

Figure 22 The incised meanders of the San Juan River near Mexican Hat, Utah. In the downcutting there appears to have been no effective tendency to move laterally.

many locations that the main channel has occupied at some time in the past are prominent. The channel seems to have moved many times as it developed the broad floodplain. The river splits into two more streams in some reaches and small channels have small meanders whose sizes are proportional to the flow carried in that reach. The white zones are gravel point bars located principally on the convex side of the river bend. Abandoned bends, former channels, and oxbow sloughs are common.

In contrast, Figure 22 shows the meanders of the San Juan River near Mexican Hat, Utah. The initial pattern of the paleoriver has been preserved through thousands of years during which the landscape was

Figure 23 A meltwater stream on the surface of the Aletch Glacier in Switzerland. The channels typically assume a meandering pattern though essentially no sediment load is being carried.

uplifted by mountain-building forces, and the river incised itself into the rising plateau. During this time there apparently was little or no tendency for the bends to move laterally and build point bars. The reasons for these differences in rate of lateral movement are unknown. The rocks into which the San Juan became incised are not as hard and resistant to erosion as the preCambrian rocks of the lower Grand Canyon, yet the bends did not change shape over an immense period of time.

It is typical for channels melted into the surface of a glacier to be of the meandering pattern, as illustrated by Figure 23, a stream on the Aletch Glacier of Switzerland. The occurrence of meanders in channels

Figure 24 The Mississippi River near St. Louis, Missouri, is an example of a sinuous channel with stable islands. (Photo by Charles B. Belt Jr.)

that carry little or no sediment demonstrates that the curvilinear form stems from hydrodynamic forces independent of the load in transport.

The other patterns, sinuous and braided, are of about equal frequency but because channels are seldom straight for more than a distance equal to 10 to 20 widths, the sinuous stream is relatively common. Sinuous rivers often have islands that are quite stable through time. An example of this type is the Mississippi River that runs from Burlington, Iowa, to St. Louis. Figure 24 shows such an example looking upstream or north past the metropolitan area of St. Louis, Missouri. In this photo the width of the river is controlled by the levees that confine the channel. The river is sinuous. The famous meanders of the river are farther downstream. Stable islands can be seen in the distance.

Another important class is the braided river, or a river that has several or many channels. It is common for the braided reach to be unstable in that the position and size of the individual channels are constantly changing. The braided stream is steeper than other patterns for channels of the same size or same discharge. It is generally true that the

Figure 25 A braided reach of the Rio Grande near Santa Clara Pueblo, New Mexico. The view is downstream. Several channels are evident in the foreground with building point bars indicating a tendency toward instability and recent lateral movement.

braided river carries a larger sediment load than alternative patterns but whether the pattern is the cause or the effect of a larger sediment load has not been resolved.

As in the case of the meandering river, the braided pattern takes many forms. One example is shown in Figure 25, a photograph of the Rio Grande south of Santa Clara, New Mexico. The Black Mesa, a remnant of a lava-capped plateau, is prominent in the middle ground. The gorge starting at Otowi is in the far background. The river here is divided into at least two channels, and the many bars indicate a tendency to change by erosion and deposition, a characteristic of the braided condition. Chute cutoffs, or small channels cutting across a point bar, can be seen in several places and are another indicator of rapid change.

A common form of braided channel can be seen on fans in front of mountain canyons, on the outwash plains from a melting glacier, or in

Figure 26   A braided reach of Indian Creek near Alpine, Idaho. The river is divided into several channels that are constantly shifting. The lateral movement has recently cut off the willow-covered point in the foreground.

gravel valleys, particularly ones that have been disturbed by destruction of the original vegetation by bulldozing or logging. The braided stream in Figure 26 shows the typical broad gravel valley floor where several channels are being carved and filled in a constantly changing configuration, creating local islands that may recently have been vegetated spurs.

The ephemeral channel that carries water only during storms is not a separate type because it can be meandering, sinuous or braided. But because it is so common in the semi-arid and arid parts of the world it deserves special mention. The type is so common that there are special names for it in various countries; in Spain it is a rambla; in the middle east, a wadi; in America, an arroyo. Some are nearly pure sand. Some are pure cobble. All are relatively wide with small depth of flow; that is, a large width to depth ratio.

An example of a sandy arroyo in the American southwest shown in Figure 27 is in the headwaters of Arroyo Frijoles near Santa Fe, New

Figure 27 The sandy bed of an ephemeral channel that has water flowing about three times a year, a tributary to Arroyo Frijoles near Santa Fe, New Mexico. The view is upstream. The bank two meters above the bed is the higher of two alluvial terraces, the lower one being covered with brush at the level of the man's waist; he is standing on the floodplain.

Mexico. Measurements show that during the few times there is water in the arroyo, perhaps three times a year, the flow scours the bed to a depth of about 15 cm while the total water depth is only 40 cm. Such a channel does not display a pool-riffle sequence; the channel is quite smooth and devoid of deep holes.

The bankfull stage and the floodplain

Most creeks or rivers flow in a definite channel bordered on one or both sides by a flat area or valley floor. With the exception of some mountain streams, nearly every river has areas that fit this description. These channels are seldom straight; bends or curves in a channel have an important effect on the manner of flow and the channel capacity.

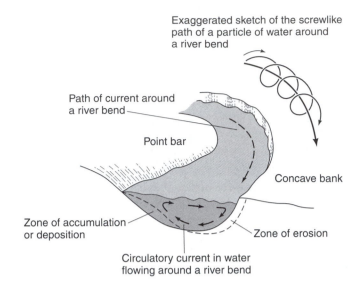

Figure 28 Effect of a curved channel on the water flow; a circulation in the cross section is produced in which surface water has a component of flow toward the concave bank.

As a flowing stream enters a bend in its channel, as shown in Figure 28, the water at the surface, being swifter than that near the bottom, moves toward the concave bank and tends to erode it. Continuity requires, then, that surface water plunge downward near the concave bank and that some bed water emerge at the surface near the convex bank. This circulatory motion in the cross-sectional plane of a channel, which was first observed and explained by Thomson in 1879, is a result of the larger centrifugal force that is exerted on fast-moving surface parcels than on slower-moving ones near the bed. The motion gives to an individual water parcel a path resembling a helix.

The water near the bottom usually is carrying along some clay, sand, or pebbles, and these are carried toward the inside of the curve by the slower-moving water. As indicated by the small arrows in the cross section shown in Figure 28, water near the surface tends to move toward the concave bank and bed water tends to move toward the convex bank of the point bar. Thus, material accumulates on the convex edge of the bend and builds up the bed on that side, giving it a gradual slope. Such deposition results in the building point bar, the top surface of which is the floodplain.

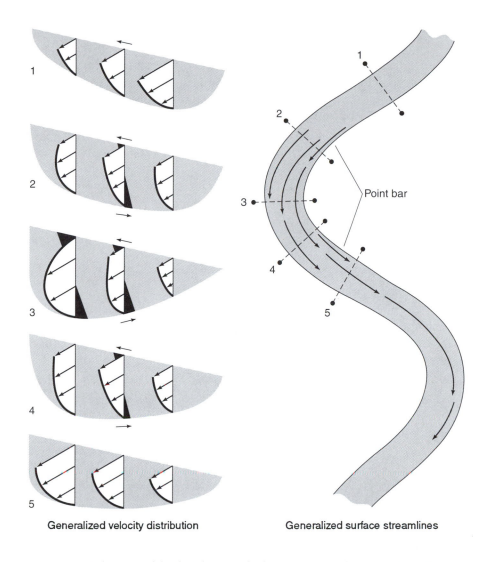

Generalized velocity distribution   **Generalized surface streamlines**

Point bar

Figure 29   A diagram of the distribution of velocity in a curved channel. Velocity increases with distance from the bed and is greatest in the deepest section.

The flow pattern of a meander is shown in Figure 29. The isometric view shows the two principal components of velocity at various positions in the bend. Because of the scale of the diagrams, the super elevation of the water surface in the bend is not shown but is implied by the velocity distribution.

The velocities in a meander crossover, or point of inflection, are not symmetrical. As would be expected, proceeding downstream from the axis of the bend, the thread of maximum velocity is much closer to the concave bank than to the center of the channel. Moreover, the high velocity continues to hug this side through the point of inflection of the curve. In narrow channels, a cross-channel velocity component is directed toward the convex bank or point bar near the bed and toward the concave bank near the surface.

The accretion of material on the point bar gradually pushes the convex bank into the channel and this tendency is compensated by the tendency of the concave bank to erode. Thus it is usual for a river channel gradually to migrate laterally across the valley floor. During such lateral migration the channel width remains the same.

If material is eroded off one bank of a channel and is deposited on the opposite bank, the channel moves gradually sideways. Because in most channels the bends are somewhat irregularly distributed along the length of the stream and the bends consist of curves both to the right and to the left, the progressive sideways movement of the channel is to the left in one place and to the right in another. Thus, given sufficient time, the channel eventually will occupy every position within the valley; each sideward motion leaves a flat or nearly level deposit that was caused by deposition on the inside of the curve. Thus the floodplain is formed.

When one looks across a flat valley floor, even a very wide one, it must be recognized that the river has at some time in the past occupied each and every position across the wide expanse, for that is the process by which the flat valley was formed.

The present course of most rivers has not changed substantially in the past hundred years, but perhaps 500 years ago the channel was in quite a different place in the valley. Such movement is natural and results from the slow erosion on one side of a bend and the deposition on the opposite side. Former positions of a river are often indicated by the moon-shaped or oxbow lakes that exist on many floodplains.

The floodplain is formed to a great extent by this deposition. In addition, some material is deposited by floods on top of the floodplain. When the river is in flood and water spreads over most of the whole valley floor, sediment carried by the water is deposited in a thin layer over the surface. Though both of these two processes operate, the extension of point bars accounts for most of the material making up the floodplain.

The floodplain is formed by the material deposited on the convex side or the inside of channel bends and the material deposited when the

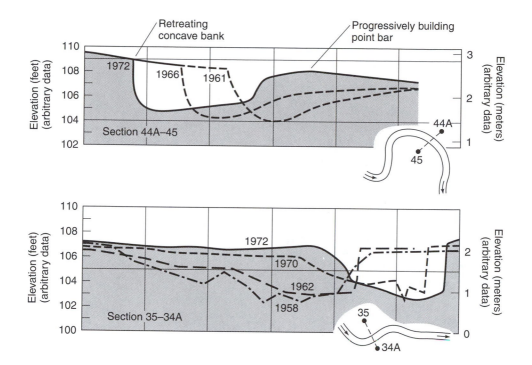

Figure 30 Measurements of the movement of the channel from 1958 to 1972 at monumented cross sections on Watts Branch, near Rockville, Maryland. During these 14 years, the channel moved an amount about equal to its width. The point bar building on the convex bank is extending the floodplain.

river overflows its banks. On top of the bedrock or material undisturbed by the river, the valley is covered with material deposited by the river. Such material usually is a mixture of sand and silt, with some gravel (Figure 19d).

There are instances where a meander bend persists for a long time, even many thousands of years, with virtually no point bar building and no appreciable lateral movement of the channel. The reason for this phenomenon is obscure, but the San Juan River provides an example of it in Figure 22.

The building of a point bar balanced by bank erosion on the opposite side of the stream is demonstrated by a series of observations of Watts Branch, a small stream near Rockville, Maryland, for which cross sections were surveyed regularly over a 41-year period. Selected examples are presented in Figure 30.

The upper diagram of Figure 30 shows successive positions of the channel during an 11 year period. It can be seen how the nearly flat sur-

Figure 31 Point bar building on the convex bank of a curve on the Colorado River at Unkar Rapid, Arizona. Just upstream of the rapid, the water depth was measured as 15 meters and the surface velocity as 3.7 meters per second.

face of the point bar (right side of the channel) is built by deposition, tending to force the channel to the left bank, which is the concave bank on a bend. The lower diagram shows an example of channel movement that is accompanied by the construction of a flat floodplain on the left bank.

Another example of point bar building along the convex bank is shown in the aerial photograph of the Colorado River at Unkar Rapid in the Grand Canyon (Figure 31). The view is looking upstream. The point bars are the light colored sandy areas on the convex bank, dotted with brushy vegetation. The upper of the two bars is entirely the deposit of sandy debris from upstream, but the near one obtained part of its form from material emanating from the side canyon in the lower left part of the photo.

The manner in which a channel moves across the valley floor, eroding one bank and building a nearly flat floodplain on the other, while
maintaining a cross section approximately constant in shape and size,
is an aspect of the dynamic equilibrium that characterizes many channel systems. Erosion on one bank and deposition on the other are approximately equal on the average, and gradual movement of the channel over the whole valley takes place without any appreciable change
in the size of the channel. The channel is constantly shifting position,
though slowly, and the valley floor, or floodplain, is the result of this
shifting. The rate of channel shifting is related to the rate at which bedload is being transported in the reach. Channel shifting is a natural,
necessary part of river behavior.

In most regions of the world, daily rainfall is the exception, not the
rule. Light rains occur more frequently than do moderate ones; a heavy
downpour occurs infrequently. A river channel will have only a moderate or small amount of water flowing in it on most days. On a few days
each year there is usually sufficient rain or snowmelt to raise the river
to a peak that just fills the channel but does not overtop its banks. The
great rates of flow that cause the largest floods occur very seldom. The
river channel is shaped by and sized to the more frequent, moderate
flows. Overflow of the floodplain accommodates the water of major
floods that cannot be carried within the channel.

Figure 32 shows a cross section of an average river and some of the
flows that can be expected at different intervals. Figure 32a shows the
river at average flow. During approximately 90 days of the year, there
is no more water than is shown in 32a. A heavy rainfall is required to
produce enough surface runoff to fill the channel to the top of the
banks. Such rains occur approximately twice each year. The level of the
water, or bankfull flow, that might be expected at twice a year is shown
in Figure 32b.

Less frequently, a storm will occur that will cause the river to flow
over the floodplain or valley flat. Approximately once every 2 years the
river will overflow the floodplain to a depth shown in Figure 32c,
which is equal to the usual depth of water in the channel at average
flow, shown in Figure 32a.

The heaviest, least frequent flows cover the floodplain even deeper.
The largest flood expected in a period of 50 years (Figure 32e) would
be required to flood the whole floodplain to a depth equal to the height
of the stream bank exposed by average flow.

The concept of the bankfull condition or bankfull discharge is simple enough. The river channel tends to be bordered by a floodplain that
has been constructed by the river as it moves laterally. The bankfull

82

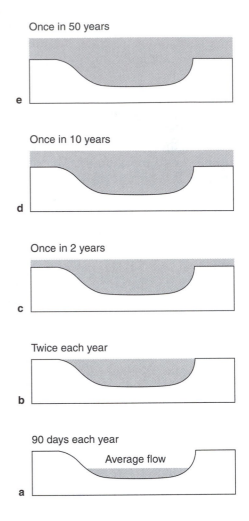

Figure 32 Amount of water in a river channel and frequency with which such an amount occurs.

condition is reached when water exceeds channel capacity and begins to flow over the floodplain. Because the floodplain is formed by extension of point bars, the top of the point bar is the best field indicator of the bankfull level. Because the river reaches bankfull only a few days each year, field observations of such flow are uncommon. Bankfull discharge is illustrated in Figure 33.

The bankfull level is often difficult to locate exactly in those many reaches or localities where the floodplain is very narrow and often obscure. There are many reaches where point bars are not well developed

Figure 33 Discharge at bankfull, an event that occurs only for a few minutes on a small stream once or twice a year. In the background water is flowing over the point bar and is beginning to cut across the point bar. In the foreground the point bar is partly covered; Watts Branch near Rockville, Maryland.

and when at some time, the point bar surface has been locally eroded or subject to deposition on its surface so that the simple idea of identifying the top of the point bar is not applicable. The bankfull level can be confused with a low terrace or abandoned floodplain such that the valley flat is not presently under construction but is a product of a previous flow regimen. Finally, floodplains are not necessarily flat and uniform but can be traversed by subtle swales or by the presence of natural levees bordering the channel and remnant features of previous channel positions.

Channels in mountainous areas are often in deep notches, especially in terrain that is influenced by tectonic uplift or alteration. Such V-shaped valleys, large or small, are seen in many regions including parts of the Rocky Mountains, the Cascade ranges, and others. In such valleys the floodplain is often either very narrow or indefinite.

In the coast range of California, though valley floors may be wide and flat, the channel is deeply incised in the alluvium deposited by the same river during a previous period. The incised channel may have only a narrow or incipient floodplain.

Bankfull level is simple in concept but often difficult to locate exactly in the field. Why is the concept important? First, the bankfull condition, though occurring only a few days a year, is the "channel forming" or "channel maintaining" flow. Data demonstrated that over a period of years, the largest amount of sediment is carried by discharges near bankfull. The so-called "effective discharge" that carries the most sediment is closely coincident with the bankfull condition.

Second, the bankfull condition is the only morphologic or channel shape parameter that coincides with a nearly constant recurrence interval of flow. For a majority of rivers, the largest discharge in a year will equal or exceed bankfull 2 out of 3 years. In terms of number of days the condition is equalled or exceeded it is usually 2 to 4 days in a year. The same recurrence interval, about 1.5 years, is seen in rivers on which the high flow is derived from spring snowmelt as well as those rivers experiencing high flows from rainstorm events. In contrast to a nearly constant recurrence interval of overflow of the floodplain, former levels of the river shown by terraces or abandoned floodplains have no consistent frequency of overflow.

One of the most important aspects of the bankfull discharge is that no bedload moves at flows much below bankfull. Nearly all the important transportation of the coarse part of the sediment load occurs during the relatively few days each year when the river is flowing near bankfull.

The frequency or number of days each year during which a river flows at a particular magnitude of flow is shown on a flow duration curve in Figure 34. The data are values of average flow for one day, or the average daily discharge. The data are the average values for 18 gaging stations located in the Front Range of Colorado and the average of stations in the Salmon River basin in Idaho. The ordinate of a duration curve may be in values of discharge per unit of time, but for many purposes it is useful to plot dimensionless values, usually the ratio of a particular discharge to the bankfull discharge. The latter is used in Figure 34. The abscissa is percentage of time. Added to the graph is a scale at the top showing number of days in a year.

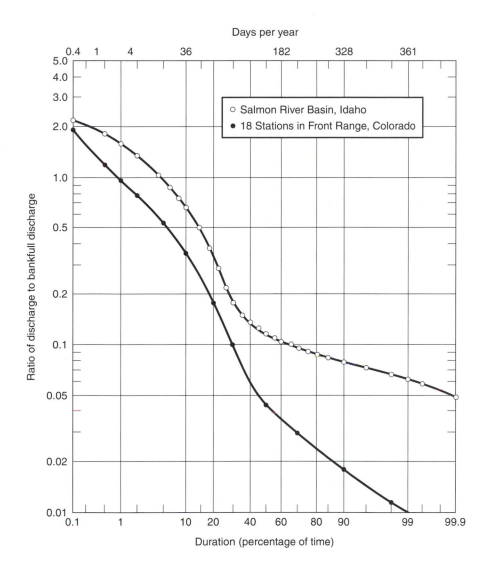

Figure 34   Duration curves of flow showing what percent of time or how many days a year the discharge is equal to, less than, or greater than bankfull. These are average curves representing many gaging stations in each region. (Adapted from Leopold, *A View of the River*, 1994, Harvard University Press, Cambridge, MA.)

At an ordinate value of unity, the discharge is equal to bankfull. The curve for the Colorado stations goes through a discharge ratio of one, or bankfull, at a percentage of time equal to one percent of 365 days. The bankfull stage for these stations is equalled or exceeded on the average of 3.6 days in a year.

The Salmon rivers stations are bankfull about 4 percent of the time or 14 days a year. At an abscissa value of 0.3 percent or one day a year, the Idaho streams have a discharge 2 times bankfull and the Colorado stations a discharge 1.5 times bankfull. The curve for the Colorado stations is quite typical and that for Idaho somewhat higher than for most rivers. It is usual for the bankfull condition to be equalled or exceeded 2 to 5 days per year.

The mean annual discharge of most rivers plots on the duration curve at about the 25 percent value. That is, the mean annual discharge is equalled or exceeded 91 days a year. This means that the flow is less than the mean annual value 273 days a year. The mean annual flow is a relatively high discharge value, typically 0.03 to 0.14 of the bankfull value.

The joining of tributaries

Small creeks join to form larger streams. Large rivers are formed by the joining of rivers of intermediate size. As tributaries meet a master stream, the discharge, width, and depth of the main river increase.

The pattern of this joining is much like the branching of a tree. Surprisingly, however, this successive merging is highly organized and is one of the many aspects of dynamic equilibrium that is maintained within the river system.

The high degree of organization may be illustrated by a network analysis, one of the several contributions of Robert E. Horton. Let the size of a river be designated by its order, here defined. A stream of first order is one that has no tributaries. When two streams of first order join, a stream segment of second order begins that may have one or several first-order tributaries along its length. However, when two streams of second order join, a single stream of third order begins. This stream extends until joined by another third-order river, and there, the fourth order begins.

The simplest way to make a network analysis is to place a piece of tracing paper over a topographic map and trace all the blue lines, thus eliminating the many other features shown on the topographic quad-

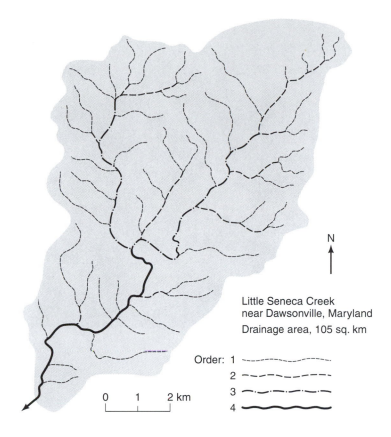

N

Little Seneca Creek
near Dawsonville, Maryland
Drainage area, 105 sq. km

Order: 1
2
3
4

0   1   2 km

Figure 35   Channel network of Little Seneca Creek above Dawsonville, Maryland. Stream orders are indicated by different symbols.

rangle. The traced net can then be analyzed by the rules presented above, each stream segment colored according to order number.

Figure 35 shows the network for part of the drainage basin of Little Seneca Creek in Maryland. Figure 36 is a photograph of that river at low and at high discharge.

After the order numbers are assigned, the length of each segment can be measured and then recorded both in a table and beside the respective segments on the map. The number and mean length of the segments of each order can then be computed. The average lengths of various orders for the two main branches of Little Seneca Creek that join just upstream of the Dawsonville gaging station are plotted on semilogarithmic paper in Figure 37. On inspection of such a graph, the nature of the geometric progression becomes clear.

Figure 36 The channel of Seneca Creek at Dawsonville, Maryland, at low flow (top) and near bankfull (bottom), looking downstream.

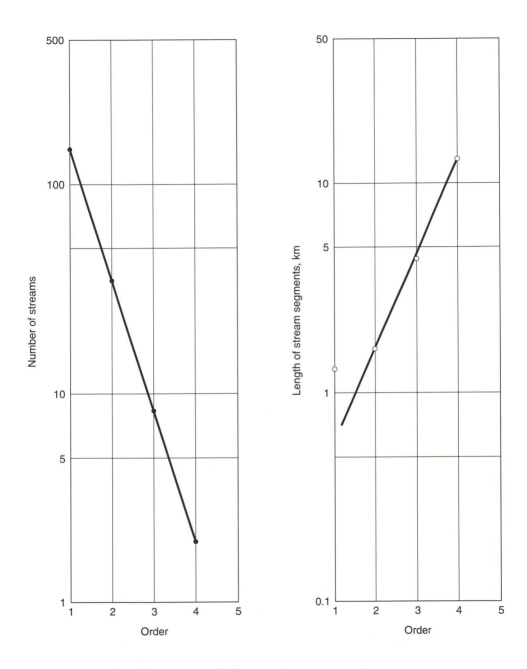

Figure 37   Plots of average stream lengths and number of streams as functions of stream order, Seneca Creek above Dawsonville, Maryland.

Note the tendency for straight-line plots. As the drainage basin size increases, the variability is diminished and plots are more nearly straight. As shown in this example, in a basin as small as a few hundred square kilometers, the average length of first-order segments is often aberrant, large relative to the lengths for streams of higher order.

The geometric relations among the lengths, slopes, order numbers, and drainage areas of tributaries show the highly organized character of river systems. For example, the straight line relating number of streams as a function of order indicates a constant ratio of number of streams of a given order to the number of the next higher order. In the plot for Little Seneca Creek, there are 4.6 times as many first-order as second-order streams. This value is within the usual range of 3.5 to 4.5.

Interestingly, when a similar analysis is made of the branching of trees, nearly the same ratio is found. Analysis of some ash trees and fir trees gave average values of 5.1 for branches and 3.2 for tree roots. The plotted data for trees in Figure 38 look very similar to the graphs in Figure 37 for a river. In both the tree branching and in river networks, I have postulated that the systems tend toward a minimization of energy expenditure; in other words, they tend toward a certain efficiency. Michael Woldenberg has studied the branching structure of blood vessels in bovine livers and in other mammalian body structures and has compared them with tree branching. He concluded, as I did, that this organization derives from a compromise between maximum probability and minimum work. This seems to be a basis for the quasi-equilibrium state in many natural systems, including rivers.

The ratio of the number and lengths of branches of various orders is a pattern that tends to minimize total length and closely approximates the network that would result from entirely random joining. Thus branching patterns of trees, rivers, blood vessels in animal tissue, and other natural networks are similarly designed for efficiency and stability.

The drainage network is important because of the obvious relation of channel size to the drainage area contibuting to a given point on the river. The magnitude of a river is a function of the contributing area. The size of the basin feeding any point in a channel system is strongly correlated with nearly every hydrologic and morphologic parameter—average flow, flood magnitude, width and depth of the channel, to name a few. Of course, channels get progressively larger as the contributing area, and thus discharge, increase.

As discharge increases downstream by the addition of tributaries, the channel width increases but not by the amount that would result

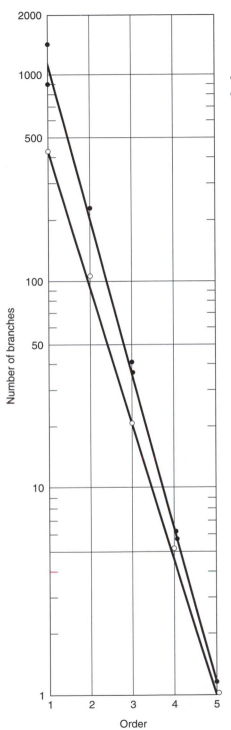

Figure 38 Plot of number of branches of different orders for some trees. Comparison with Figure 37 shows that branching patterns have much in common.

from the mere addition of the widths of the joining segments. Studies of the morphologic geometry of channels of various sizes led us to the conclusion that the channel width is proportional to the square root of the average discharge. It followed from this observation that when two streams join, the width of the combined channels would be approximately equal to the square root of the sum of squares of the widths of the separate channels. Unbeknownst to them, the observations made by Lewis and Clark provided the first data against which this hypothesis could be tested. On November 13, 1803, Lewis was taking his supplies and men down the Ohio River in preparation for the ascent up the Missouri River. He measured the width of the Ohio at its mouth as 1,274 yards, the width of the Mississippi above the junction as 1,435 yards, and the width of the combined rivers as 2,002 yards. Indeed the sum of squares is 3,682,301 and its square root is 1,918 yards, a difference of only 4 percent from the theoretical value. This says more about the amazingly accurate observations of the explorers than about any theory.

As discussed in the effect of channel storage on flood peaks, the increase in channel size downstream results in an increasing capacity to pass flood discharge without overflow. Though drainage area increases abruptly at tributary junctions, length, of course, increases continuously. It is significant, however, that about half the streams of a given order enter directly into channels two or more orders higher. There are many small, wedge-shaped areas that drain directly into a master stream, but are individually of such small size that they do not maintain even a first-order channel. The percentage of total area that so drains directly into the main channels is surprisingly high. It comprises about 20 percent of the total drainage area in basins of third and fourth order.

Flow frequency and floods

All rivers naturally experience high discharge at a time of heavy precipitation. Fluctuation of flow with time is a consequence of the sequence of stormy and nonstormy periods.

The river does not form a channel that would convey without overflow all possible flow events. In fact, the channel can contain within its banks only a discharge of modest size. The greater discharges must overflow onto the valley floor. For this reason the flat valley floor or floodplain is indeed part of the channel during unusual storms. When humans use this part of the river for construction or agriculture, they are encroaching on the river; buildings, roads, and crops may be damaged or destroyed when overflow occurs.

Floods, then, are events of such magnitude that the channel cannot accommodate the peak discharge. A flood is a flow in excess of channel capacity. It is a normal and expected characteristic of rivers. Most rivers, on the average, experience discharges in excess of bankfull capacity approximately 2 or 3 times a year.

A great, really catastrophic, flood may occur this year, next year, or the next. Such a flood might occur only once in several generations. Great floods occurred in New England in 1955 and again with hurricane Agnes, which hit the eastern United States in 1972. The floods in the United States' Midwest and upper Mississippi Valley of 1993 were truly exceptional. So extraordinary was the rainfall that fell during these disasters that it might not be repeated in another 1,000 years.

The chance of experiencing a great flood is similar to playing bridge. The game may be played often, but most players have never been dealt 13 cards of the same suit. Yet they know that they might get such a hand in the next game. So it is with floods. The very unusual event may occur tomorrow, but it is unlikely.

Floods are significant and climatically controlled events. The occurrence of floods is studied as a probability problem, and knowledge of the probability of flood occurrence is needed for a variety of engineering and economic reasons. These needs and potential uses have led to a considerable effort over many years to develop systematic procedures for analyzing flood probability. Probability studies of flood occurrence are also important tools in geomorphology.

In contrast with records of annual or monthly value of mean runoff, flood occurrences may be treated as random events because the meteorologic and hydrologic factors affecting flood production vary randomly with time sufficiently that the combinations have many characteristics of chance events. The underlying premise is that the floods occurring during a specific period constitute a sample of an indefinitely large population in time. For example, if the largest flood record in a 30-year period was of a certain size, a flood of equal magnitude will probably occur during the next 30 years.

Analysis of the annual flood begins with the tabulation of the highest discharge in each year of record at the station. Momentary peak discharges are used if they are available. The sample then includes only one event in each year. The mean of this series is called the mean annual flood.

The plotting position for individual items in the array is determined by the formula

$$\text{Recurrence interval} = \frac{N+1}{M},$$

where N equals the number of years of record and M is the rank of the individual item in the array.

The ordinate scale, discharge in cms, may be either arithmetic or logarithmic. The abscissa is recurrence interval in years. In the usual array or annual flood series, the peak discharge for each year is used in the array and it is the annual flood in the sense that it is the greatest flood event in that year. When these annual events are plotted against the recurrence interval, the interpretation of the plot is as follows: It is probable that, on the average over a period of years, the recurrence interval of an annual peak of Y cms will be X years. The use of a logarithmic scale for the ordinate tends to make the plotted graph more or less straight, but a completely straight line is neither expected nor common.

The mode of plotting and the use of such a graph can be explained by an example. Figure 39 is the flood frequency curve for Seneca Creek near Dawsonville, Maryland, plotting the annual floods in the 61-year record.

The procedure for plotting a flood frequency curve for an individual station has been improved so that various agencies or companies could obtain similar estimates from a given set of data. Development of the improved method, carried out by the Hydrologic Subcommittee of the Interagency Advisory Committee on Water Data, is based on the finding that the observed data plot best on a Pearson Type III distribution using a log transformation. The skew coefficient of the station record is weighted by the pooled information from nearby stations. This method now is widely used in hydrologic practice.

For developing a flood frequency curve for an ungaged location, a regional analysis is made using many gaging stations in a region. Because different gaging stations have different drainage areas and thus produce different magnitudes of flood peak for a rainstorm of a given size, it is necessary to reduce the records to a common base that takes out the effect of drainage basin size. This is done by expressing the discharge values as ratios to the mean annual flood.

This type of regional flood frequency analysis has been improved by the use of various physical characteristics of the drainage basin to develop a different equation for the discharges associated with each

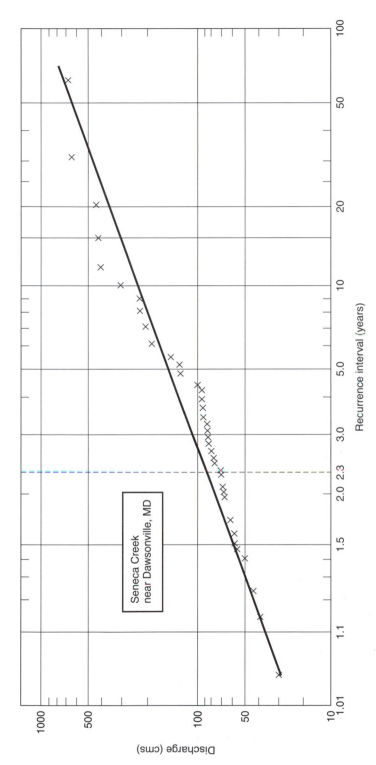

Figure 39 Flood frequency curve for 61-year record at Seneca Creek at Dawson-ville, Maryland. It is a plot of the annual floods, that is the highest instantaneous discharge each year of record. (Adapted from Leopold, *A View of the River*, 1994, Harvard University Press, Cambridge, MA.)

Recurrence interval (years)

Discharge (cms)

Seneca Creek
near Dawsonville, MD

quantile of recurrence interval, 1.2, 2.33, 5, 10, 25, 50 years. Physical parameters used in multiple correlation include those most important in reducing standard error, which in order of decreasing importance are: drainage area, channel slope, surface storage such as lakes, rainfall intensity, January temperature, and orographic influences. This method was developed by M. A. Benson and has been used in many regional analyses published by the U.S. Geological Survey.

The mean annual flood is the arithmetic mean of the annual flood peaks. Each annual flood is divided by the mean annual flood and the quotient is plotted against the recurrence interval. A typical plot of "ratio to mean annual flood" versus "recurrence interval" is shown on page 9 of the U.S. Geological Survey's *Water Supply Paper 1672*, which is applicable to the region that includes Little Seneca Creek at Dawsonville, Maryland. Similar analyses for other parts of the United States are published in *Water Supply Papers 1671 to 1688*.

The mean annual flood has, on the average, a recurrence interval of 2.3 years; that is, once every 2.3 years on the average, the highest flow of the year will equal or exceed the value of the mean annual flood. On plotted graphs of flood frequency as in Figure 39, the recurrence interval for the mean annual flood is shown as a vertical dashed line at the value of 2.3 years on the abscissa scale.

The very important value of the bankfull discharge can be read from the flood frequency curve at the recurrence interval of 1.5 years. But before examining that estimate, the actual value can be obtained in the field at a place where a channel geometry survey has been done. In such a field examination, we make a leveling survey across the floodplain and determine its elevation. At the Seneca Creek gage, the floodplain is well exhibited as the valley flat at the top of the left bank in the photographs of Figure 36 where it is nearly 60 meters wide on the left bank but is represented by only a narrow berm or flat place on the right bank.

From the surveyed cross section, the channel is approximately 15 m wide at the base and 21 m wide at the top and the bankfull stage corresponds to a gage height of 1.6 m. If the rating curve at that gage height is entered, the corresponding discharge value is approximately 43 cms. If the flood frequency curve at a recurrence interval of 1.5 years is entered in Figure 39, the discharge value is about 55 cms. This is in rough agreement with the bankfull discharge estimated from field inspection of the channel cross section and reading from the rating curve.

Thus, the channel of Seneca Creek at the station has a capacity of approximately 43 cms without overflow; this is the bankfull discharge.

Many peak discharges are higher than that figure, and of course many may be lower. Sixty-one events in the period 1931–1961 equaled or exceeded bankfull. This means that there were, on the average, 2 flows per year that were equal to or greater than bankfull. A figure of two flows per year is the average for most rivers.

A river flowing at bankfull will not be at the overflow level everywhere along the channel because there are always slight variations in height of bank or depth of channel.

Shown in the photograph of Figure 33 is a channel at bankfull, a reach of Watts Branch near Rockville, Maryland. Note that the flat area in the foreground is a point bar that is just being overflowed. Immediately upstream, in the middle of the photograph, the flow is cutting over a point bar in what is called a neck cutoff. Photographs taken at the bankfull stage or when the floodplain is just being covered with water are rare, for the momentary situation is quickly gone.

The causes of floods—small basins

Discharges large enough to overtop the river banks and flow over the floodplain are common. Precipitation, sometimes combined with snowmelt, is often sufficient to cause overbank flows, but resulting runoff can be greatly enhanced by several circumstances. Previous wetting of the ground surface prior to the flood-producing precipitation is a common cause of unusual discharge. Infiltration rate is decreased by soil wetting and so a given rainfall event produces more runoff and a higher peak rate if it falls on a previously wetted surface. In the extreme case of soil saturation, all the rainfall becomes surface runoff. Soil saturation can be caused by prolonged precipitation. Zero infiltration can also result from freezing of the wetted surface.

High runoff rates are importantly related to intensity of rainfall and to various factors influencing the speed of concentration of runoff water, particularly influences due to human activity. Rainfall intensity is an important determinant of peak discharge. For example, the runoff rate resulting from two centimeters of rain in a day is quite different from the peak rate if two centimeters fell in half an hour.

Human influences on peak runoff rates from small basins are manifested in two ways. First, many activities such as grazing by animals, deforestation, surface paving, or agricultural practices decrease infiltration. Second, alterations in surface conditions such as many aspects of urbanization including roof downspouts, street gutters, and storm sewerage speed the movement of surface water downslope and down-channel. These influxes affect peak discharges from relatively small basins and thus are important to municipal water handling projects and to agricultural areas where small streams cause important damage to crops and to infrastructure. But great floods on large rivers are caused by great storms, widespread rapid snowmelt, and are essentially uninfluenced by forests, agricultural practices or urbanization.

The effects of urbanization and alteration of the land surface may be quantified by their effect on the speed with which rain water moves downstream. This is measured by the lag time or the time in hours between the center of mass of the rain and the center of mass of the runoff measured at some point down the channel. Roof downspouts, sheet gutters, storm sewerage all tend to speed the movement of water and thus shorten the lag between rainfall and runoff. If a given volume of runoff must be discharged in a shorter period of time, then the peak discharge must be higher. This is shown in the graphs of Figure 40. The area under the hydrograph is the volume of runoff because it is the product of a discharge rate multiplied by time. The areas under the original and after-urbanization hydrographs are equal but the peak has increased due to the decreased lag time.

A quantitative example is the storm of February 15, 1984, on the 17.6 hectare basin of Cerrito Creek near Berkeley, California, which is shown in Figure 41. The low-intensity rain prior to 10:30 did not produce runoff but a rain burst of 8.2 mm between 10:30 and 11:00 resulted in a runoff of 0.39 mm. The peak discharge came 10 minutes after the burst of rain and the lag time to the center of runoff was 0.22 hours. The measured peak was 1.6 mm per hour.

Discharge is volume per unit of time, often expressed as cubic meters per second, cms. But volume may also be given as depth over a specified area, usually as millimeters. For example, 1 mm over 1 hectare is the volume of 10 cubic meters, and 1 mm/hr from 1 hectare is 10 cubic meters per hour or 0.0028 cms. The use of mm/hr is a convenient unit in hydrology because it expresses both the rate of rainfall and the rate of runoff.

Many observations of individual rainstorms at various locations led to the development of a relationship between lag time and drainage area for natural and undisturbed basins. From this curve the expected lag for a basin the size of Cerrito Creek before urbanization can be read. The lag would have been 0.47 hours under natural or unurbanized conditions. The peak rainfall that would have occurred under the condition of natural lag time is 0.76 mm per hour. Thus, the decreased

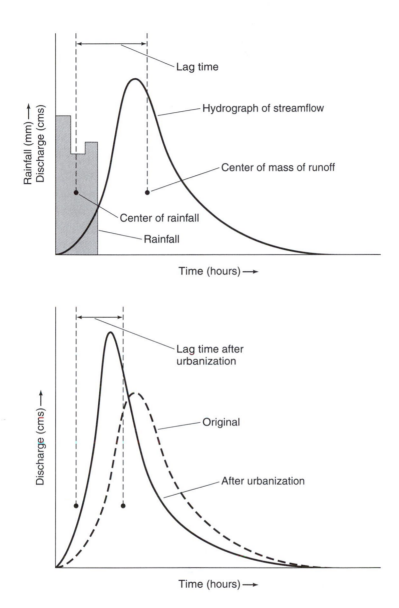

Figure 40 Hypothetical hydrographs relating runoff to rainfall, showing the effect of decreased lag time on flood peak. (After Leopold, *A View of the River*, 1994, Harvard University Press, Cambridge, MA.)

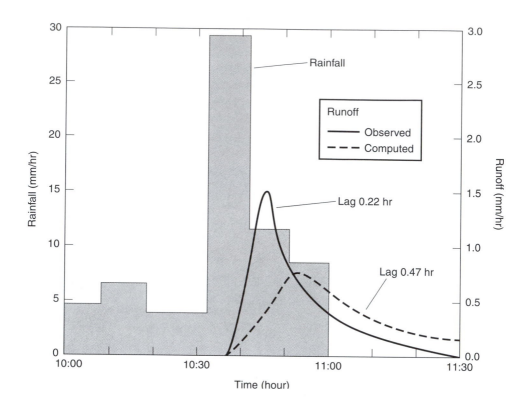

Figure 41 Measured rainfall and resulting runoff in a storm burst February 15, 1984, on Cerrito Creek, Berkeley, California. Shown in dashed line is the computed hydrograph representing the flow from the same storm when the basin was in natural condition before urbanization.

lag alone or speeding runoff increased the peak flow by a factor of two. From other storms and basins in the same area, computation shows that land surface altered by urbanization and exotic vegetation increased the peak flow by as much as 8 times.

The causes of floods—large basins

Great floods in large rivers are but little influenced by land use on the basin. They result from unusual combinations of continued rainfall over a large area, frozen ground on the watershed, snowmelt and/or extraordinary total amounts of rainfall. When the ground surface of a

100

large basin is soaked by continuous rain or is frozen, infiltration is reduced in importance and the stage is set for a high percentage of precipitation discharging as surface runoff. Under such conditions of low or minimum infiltration, the usual effect of good vegetative cover becomes negligible and nearly all rainfall immediately becomes surface runoff.

Human intervention can compensate for the lack of storage in the soil by the construction of reservoirs. However, reservoir storage for flood control exerts its influence immediately downstream from the reservoir and its ameliorating effect on flood peaks decreases rapidly with distance downstream. This is the result of two circumstances. First, storage in the channel itself acts on a flood wave much like the reservoir action that decreases flood peak while spreading the runoff through a longer time period.

An example of how a flood hydrograph changes as the water flows downstream was shown in Figure 18. The flow spreads out over a longer time as the peak progresses downstream. This spreading decreases the peak discharge.

The second reason that reservoirs reduce peak discharge primarily near the dam is that tributaries entering downstream of the dam may produce flood discharge from areas not controlled by the dam. The contribution of drainage area downstream of a dam is well illustrated by the 1993 floods in the upper Mississippi River basin. The several big dams on the Missouri River did not prevent devastation in the lower reaches of the Missouri.

The 1993 floods of the upper Mississippi were notable in several respects. The conditions leading to the wide-spread overflows exemplify the cause of great floods in the center of continental areas. There were exceptional rainfalls both in amount, in area covered, and in duration. But of greatest importance was the timing of flood peaks from several large tributaries that produced record-high discharge at their locus of convergence. Millions of acres of land were inundated and unofficial estimates of damage exceeded $10 billion.

There had been an exceptionally high rainfall total in the area centered in Iowa and nearby states during the fall and winter before the flood. This area experienced the second wettest November to April in 121 years of record. Then came a period in June 1993 when 50 to 178 mm of rain fell in northern Iowa. This was followed by two storms in July, when 50 to 200 mm of rain fell. In the period July 22 to 24, 50 to 330 mm of rain fell in parts of Nebraska, Kansas, Missouri, Iowa, and Illinois. The early July storms led to peak discharges in the Skunk, Raccoon, and Des Moines river basins that converged on the Mississippi at the same time that high discharge from the upper Mississippi River moved toward its junction with the Missouri River. This resulted in a peak discharge at St. Louis that was greater than any flood since 1844.

A graphic example of the magnitude of water volume that fell in a short period of time was estimated from maps of precipitation in southern Iowa during the two days of July 4–5, 1993. In those 2 days, about 54,000 square kilometers received over 25 mm of rain. An area of about 388 square kilometers received more than 178 mm in the same period of time. The total volume of rain is estimated at 4.44 cubic kilometers. This amount nearly equals the storage volume behind Shasta Dam, California. It is nearly double the capacity of Elephant Butte Reservoir, New Mexico. It is about one fifth the capacity of Lake Powell behind Glen Canyon Dam, Arizona.

With such a vast amount of water falling in just two days it is hardly surprising that in Iowa alone, 27 gaging stations experienced discharges exceeding values expected once in 100 years, that is values with an annual probability of less than 0.01. The Mississippi River flood of 1973 was slightly less severe than 1993. The peak stage at St. Louis in 1973 was 43 feet (13.1 m) and in 1993 49 feet (14.9 m), a difference of nearly two meters. Figure 42 shows the extensive flooding just above St. Louis on April 28, 1973.

It is logical to ask how such extraordinary discharges affect the river channel. Is the channel washed away, destructively eroded, or completely altered? At most locations little change was observed. Similarly little change in channel morphology was observed on the small basin, 9.6 square kilometers, of Watts Branch, Maryland, where an extensive array of surveyed cross sections was installed. In 1972 the basin experienced the largest discharge on record as a result of Hurricane Agnes. A cross section that was surveyed just before and just after the flood showed so little change that the difference was within the usual limit of survey accuracy. As discussed previously, it is the modest but frequent flows that shape, alter, and maintain the channel morphology.

Channel history—river terraces

Erosional forces acting on an uplifted land mass tend to reduce its elevation through time. Rivers as well as hillslopes tend to downcut gradually, while maintaining certain relationships along the river length. But the rate of downcutting is generally slow enough to allow processes of lateral movement of the channel to operate, thus resulting

Figure 42 The flood of April 28, 1973, looking upstream to the junction of the Missouri and Mississippi. The Missouri flows from left background to right middleground. The Mississippi channel is marked by the lines of trees; the white road is on top of the left bank levee. (Photo by Charles B. Belt Jr.)

in the formation of floodplains in the valleys of most rivers and creeks. These floodplains vary in width, depending on the size of the river, the relative rates of downcutting, and the hardness or resistance of the rock material of the valley walls. Floodplains may occur in the valleys of creeks or torrents even a few feet wide but are generally absent along most headwater tributaries, presumably because downcutting is sufficien ly rapid that time is not sufficient for lateral movement of any magnitude.

Floodplains tend to be absent from most headwater channels but often appear at the point where flow in the channel changes from ephemeral to perennial—that is, where groundwater enters the channel in sufficient quantity to sustain flow throughout nonstorm periods. Perennial flow is influential in promoting rock weathering along the stream margin and sloughing into the channel, thus promoting lateral deposition and erosion along the stream.

During any period, then, when climatic characteristics remain approximately constant, and in the absence of uplift or change of base

Figure 43   The gully of the Rio Puerco del Oeste at Manuelito, New Mexico. The previous flood plain is now the top of a terrace six meters above the streambed. The stream is making a new meandering channel within the confines of the terrace walls.

level, downcutting is slow enough that lateral swinging of the channel can usually make the valley wider than the channel itself. However, the elevation of the channel can be changed episodically because of alteration of tectonic, mountain-building and climatic factors.

In such a circumstance the floodplain level previously associated with the stream is abandoned, either by downcutting or by aggradation. During downcutting the previous floodplain is dissected, and portions may remain as continuous benches bordering the river or, more often, as remnants of flat or nearly flat spurs jutting into the river valley. An example is shown in Figure 43—the valley of the Rio Puerco del Oeste near Manuelito, New Mexico. The broad valley flat was formerly the floodplain but it was dissected by downcutting of the river and is presently a terrace.

A terrace is defined as an abandoned floodplain. A terrace is composed of two parts, the scarp and the stair tread above and behind it. The term "terrace" is usually applied to both the scarp and the flat tread—that is, to the whole feature of the landscape. "Terrace" is sometimes used to include or to mean the deposit itself, when alluvium rather than bedrock underlies the tread and riser, but the deposit should more properly be referred to as a fill, alluvial fill, or alluvial deposit, to differentiate it from the topographic form.

The floodplain is defined as the flat area bordering a stream, constructed by the river in the present climate and inundated during periods of high flow. Because the floodplain is built by the river, it is underlain by alluvial material, that is, material deposited by running water. Alluvial fill, in the present context, is a deposit of unconsolidated or partially consolidated river-laid material in a stream valley. It is a single stratigraphic unit.

The stages of development of a terrace are diagrammed in Figure 44. Two possible sequences of events are shown that lead to the same surface configuration. Figure 44a shows a river flowing on a floodplain. A change of climate or tectonic (mountain-building) warping could cause the river to degrade or cut into the material on which it has been flowing. At this lower elevation, given time, lateral swinging of the channel develops a new floodplain, leaving the former floodplain as a pair of terrace remnants bordering the valley.

An alternative sequence is erosion (degradation or lowering), which is shown to occur between Figures 44c and d. This is followed by aggradation (deposition or rise of river bed elevation). After the period of degradation followed by aggradation, the valley has the same form as in Figure 44b that resulted from degradation alone.

The point to be stressed here is that a terrace is an abandoned surface not related to the present stream. The sequence of events leading to the observed features in the field may include several periods of alluvial deposition. If incision and aggradation occur repeatedly, it is possible to develop any number of terraces. Likewise, depending on the magnitude and sequence of the deposition and erosion, any number of fills of different stratigraphic units can be deposited. It should be noted that several alluvial fills can comprise the valley sediments, even when no evidence of a terrace exists.

Successive periods of erosion and deposition lead to the formation of river terraces and subsequent dissection. Such a sequence thus provides a method of reconstructing a history of past events that is especially useful in archaeology. The relation of the artifacts of man to their

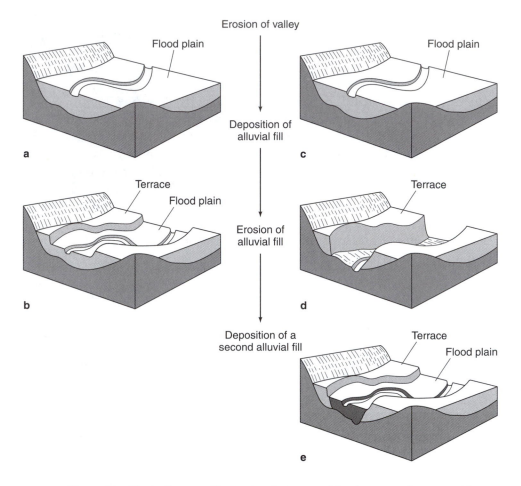

Figure 44 Block diagrams illustrating the stages of development of a terrace. Two sequences of events leading to the same surface geometry are shown in a, b, and c, d, e, respectively. (Adapted from Leopold et al., *Fluvial Processes in Geomorphology*, 1964, W. H. Freeman and Company.)

stratigraphic position in alluvial terrace deposits has been of major importance in promoting knowledge of ancient peoples. An example is in Figure 45, which illustrates the trenching of the alluvium in Coyote C. Arroyo near Tesuque, New Mexico, leaving the former valley floor as a terrace. In the photograph, I am pointing a staff at the location of a paleoindian hearth whose C14 date is 2,800 years before present. A diagrammatic cross section of the alluvial fills in this area is shown in Figure 46. In a nearby stratigraphic section, pottery shards, together with

Figure 45 An alluvial terrace in Coyote C. Arroyo near Tesuque, New Mexico. I am pointing to a location in the fill where a paleoindian hearth was exposed. Its C14 date is 2,800 years before present.

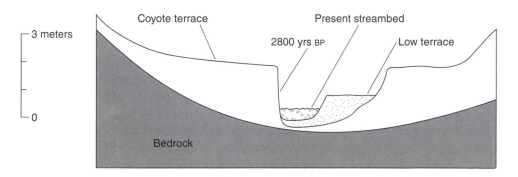

Figure 46 Generalized cross section of the alluvial sequence near Santa Fe, New Mexico. Photographs of the fills are shown in Figures 27, 45, 50.

Figure 47 Exposure of alluvial fills in the walls of the channel of Rio Puerco near Gallup, New Mexico. Three ages of deposition are seen, the most recent of which is the dark-colored silt deposited in a channel cut in the earlier fill.

C14 dates, enabled an interpretation of the relation of climatic events to occupancy by early man. Pottery remnants or shards whose dates could be determined from the design and the glaze were found deposited in the alluvial fill.

The sequence of events causing erosion and deposition can be derived from the combination of dated pottery and the relation of alluvial fills and terraces. The sequence of events can often be derived from the relation among several alluvial formations. In Figure 47 three periods of deposition can be seen in one exposure. The oldest, at the base, is

Figure 48   The alluvial terrace bordering the channel of Lance Creek near Lusk, Wyoming, stands five meters above the present channel bed. The floodplain supports grass and cottonwoods, while the terrace supports only sagebrush.

strongly bedded with horizontal layers of sand. Later it was covered by a thick layer of silt. At some time still later, a channel was eroded and that was followed by deposition of dark red clayey silt that appears dark in the photo. In the last 150 years the present channel was cut and the sequence exposed. This means that at least five changes of climate occurred in approximately the last 3,000 years.

Another example of the relation of floodplain to terrace is shown in Figure 48. In most field situations, as in this photograph, the vegetative association on the floodplain differs from that on the terrace. Here on

Figure 49 Three alluvial terraces are present in the valley of Salt Wells Creek in southern Wyoming. The three-meter-high wall in the center of the photo exposes the oldest fill; in the left center there is a two-meter wall exposing the intermediate fill covered with sage brush. A still lower terrace is not obvious in this location.

Lance Creek in eastern Wyoming, the floodplain is grassy and has groves of cottonwood trees, whereas the terrace, seen as the vertical cliff in the middle ground, is high above the local water table and supports a sagebrush cover. This is typical of many alluvial valleys of the western United States.

Another example of the relationship of terrace and floodplain, one typical of northern New Mexico and Arizona, was shown in Figure 27. The sandy channel is a tributary to the Arroyo de los Frijoles near Santa Fe, New Mexico. The low terrace stands about 1 meter above the bed of the channel and is vegetated with Atriplex bushes. It is at the level of the knees of the person in the photo. The prominent terrace, 2 meters above the streambed, is vegetated with pinon-juniper trees and grass and is easily perceived as a flat surface near the channel.

The ubiquity of these feature throughout the semi-arid states is notable. Figure 49 shows the valley of Salt Wells Creek, Wyoming, in

Figure 50 The alluvial terrace standing about two meters above the bed of Arroyo Frijoles near Santa Fe, New Mexico, is the prominent feature, but a lower, younger terrace is in the foreground.

which there are three alluvial terraces. In the middle ground of the picture is a vertical cliff that exposes the oldest of three deposits. In the left center is an intermediate height that represents a fill deposited in the channel that cut into the older material. Below that is a still lower and rather inconspicuous level—the youngest of the three alluvial deposits. The sequence is similar to that shown in Figure 47. Still another example is in Figure 50, in the Arroyo Frijoles, a tributary to the Rio Santa Fe, New Mexico. The arroyo is cut into the same alluvial Coyote formation shown in Figure 46. The person in the foreground is standing on the later low terrace.

To show some of the general uniformity of sequences that occur in widely separated areas, Figure 51 presents diagramatic cross sections

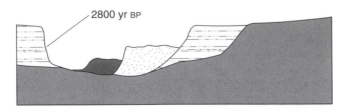

2800 yr BP

El Margo Arroyo,
Dulce, CO

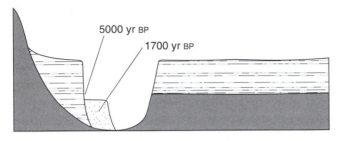

5000 yr BP

1700 yr BP

Bear Valley,
Contra Costa
County, CA

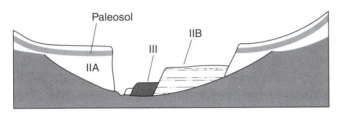

Paleosol

IIB

III

IIA

Eastern Wyoming

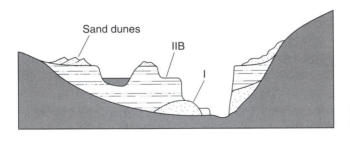

Sand dunes

IIB

I

Northeastern
Navajo country

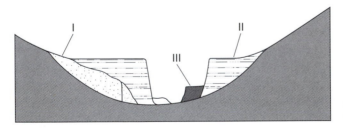

I

II

III

Central
Navajo country

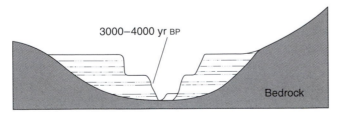

3000–4000 yr BP

Bedrock

Marin County, CA

112

Figure 51 Diagrammatic sections of alluvial valleys in various parts of the western United States show the similarity of the sequences, with three prominent Holocene terraces, the oldest of which was deposited from 3,000 to 6,000 years ago.

of the alluvial fills in various parts of the western United States. Most alluvial valleys show three terrace levels, all developed in the last 5,000 to 7,000 years of the post-glacial Holocene period and all illustrating a sequence of deposition alternating with erosion.

There are at least five levels of terraces along the Kali Gandak west of Katmandu in Nepal pictured in Figure 52. The foothills of the Himalayas dominate the right part of the photo and the incised river flows toward the camera. The rapid and periodic rise of the mountain range is well documented and it is reasonable to ascribe the formation of the terraces pictured to the uplift of the great mountain range.

Figure 52 Five terraces border the incised channel of the Kali Gandak in western Nepal. These are formed by the downcutting of the river as tectonic forces uplift the Himalayas.

By far the most prevalent cause of terrace formation is climatic change. At least two periods of exceptional climate during which incision or downcutting probably took place have been identified by geologic, stratigraphic, biologic, and dating techniques. After the retreat of glaciers about 10,000 years ago, the southwestern United States and elsewhere experienced a cool and moist period that ended with the Altithermal, a time when the climate was drier and warmer than today. The actual dates of this warm, dry episode have been confirmed by the study of the paleoindian site near Clovis, New Mexico, by Vance Haynes who determined from carbon 14 dating that the period of desiccation extended from about 8,000 to 5,000 years before present. It is believed that extensive valley erosion occurred during this dry period, leaving the former flooplain as the high terraces seen in the diagrams of Figure 51.

That period of valley erosion was followed by a long period of aggradation or valley sedimentation that again was ended by a period of desiccation sometime following the Roman period. This dry period has been dated in the American southwest by various geological studies. Scott Stine's investigations of Owens Lake and the Sierra Nevada lakes date the desiccation of southern Caifornia at 800 to 1100 AD, and indicate the occurrence of another drought beginning 50 years later and ending in 1350 AD.

These archaeological and geological studies provide a basis for explaining the repeated epicycles of erosion and deposition in the valleys of the American Southwest, a history preserved and demonstrated by the sequence of alluvial fills in the valleys.

Successive changes in rivers through the last few thousand years have significance for modern societies. The river degrades or erodes and aggrades when there is a change in the relation of runoff to sediment production. It has been postulated that if the climatic change is such that rainfall events are more intense, causing what have been called "gully washers" to be more frequent, channels erode. If on the other hand the climatic trend is toward light but frequent rains, then vegetation prospers and sediment is produced by the slow but effective process of sheet erosion on hillslopes. Channel erosion is replaced by deposition and valley alluviation occurs.

The sequence of events has implications for present land use. Human modification of the land surface operates on the hydrologic system in a manner similar to changes in climate. It is known that urbanization increases flood peaks; roads, parking lots, roofs, forest clearing, and agricultural fields laid bare of vegetation tend to increase peak flows of rivers, just as if the climate itself had changed.

Terraces provide an insight into alterations that have occurred in the past. The study of alluvial history should make us think about the landscape changes that can stem from changes in the hydrologic regime of rivers.

The riparian zone

In an ecosystem, no part stands alone. The very nature of the community is interdependence and interaction. The physical components of an ecosystem are involved with the biotic elements, for they depend in part on the biotic web and react if the biotic elements change.

So it is with rivers. They are physical components of the ecosystem in which they are embedded, and they react. It is in the riparian corridor that the interdependence of physical and biological elements is most evident. The riparian zone comprises those areas near the river channel that affect the channel and are affected by it. This zone of interaction should not be defined as having a particular width, nor is it just that margin affected by the water in the channel. Indeed, the material influence may extend far from the channel or may be limited to a narrow strip along the waterway. By looking at the nature of the interaction, this flexible definition may be better understood.

The riparian zone is characterised by its vegetation, trees, brush, grass, sedges; this zone and the river channel are interdependent. The riparian vegetation has two direct physical contributions to the river: a) it promotes bank stability, and b) its shading is a major control of water temperature. In turn, the river supports the riparian vegetation by providing water, both underground and at the surface at times of overflow. The vegetated zone along a river provides habitat for many species of fauna and flora. Narrow, linear strips of vegetation provide only "edge effect" habitat that makes organisms vulnerable to predation, parasitism, and human disturbance.

The advent of "clean" farming has led to widespread usurpation of hedgerows and riparian vegetation. Flood control works have impacted stream borders. Channelization, riprapping, and levee construction have caused permanent destruction of riparian habitat. Such areas have suffered from agricultural, industrial, and domestic demands for water that have led to a reduction of instream flow and a greater drawdown of the groundwater table. The Center for Conservation Biology stated that over 90 percent of riparian forests in the western United States have been deforested or degraded.

The interdependence of channel and riparian border has another, nonphysical aspect. The vegetation along a river channel gives the channel character and determines its aesthetic flavor. This is not a small contribution, for all people, at all levels of education, see rivers as an inherent expression of their land and landscape. This becomes clear if one thinks of the impression conveyed to a viewer by the floodplain sycamores of humid climate streams, the cottonwood islands of the Missouri and the Rio Grande, the mesquite brushland lining the arroyos of southern Arizona, or the rabbitbrush low terrace in the pinon juniper woodland of the semiarid states. Then there are the thorn bush lines along the wadis of the Negev, the towering tropical hardwoods bordering the tributaries of big rivers in Central and South America, and the dense spruces along the gravel rivers of the Alaska Range in Alaska.

In contrast, there are the overgrazed and trampled borders of overwide channels in many semi-arid areas, with channel banks broken down into sloping muddy margins. The floodplain trees have no new stems because emerging new growth is immediately grazed to the ground.

The riparian zone is an essential part of the river system and an emblem of the artistic soul of human beings.

Rivers, Creeks, and Vegetation

Soil, water, and plants

Plants grow best in dark, fine soil that crumbles easily between the fingers. Soil that is full of hard clods of light color will harden when it dries and the tender plants will not grow well. Soil differs from weathered rock in three principal ways: the presence of humus, the development of layers, and the formation of crumbs.

A good soil has plenty of humus, organic material containing small particles of decomposed plant material (originally small roots, leaves, and stems) that are broken down into bits mixed with the particles of mineral material, sand, and clay. The action of air, rain, and solutes on rocks—that is, weathering—causes decomposition into small pieces. But weathered rock without humus will not produce large, healthy plants.

The process of weathering at the earth's surface has another effect. Water passing through the surface dissolves some parts of the rock material, slowly but surely. The dissolved material, like sugar in tea, is carried by the water. Thus, the surface layer of soil material loses some ingredients, and deeper layers may gain those same ingredients. This process of movement by partial solution develops layers near the surface. Such layers can be seen in road cuts along the highway. A commonly found dark band right at the surface indicates that the uppermost layer has acquired some dark organic material, humus. The presence of humus implies that this layer has lost some mineral material by solution.

The changes accompanying this slow process of rock breakdown and development of layers also make the small individual particles of clay and silt stick together in crumbs. Between the crumbs are open

117

spaces through which water may filter down. The accumulation of small particles into crumbs forms the structure of a soil. Humus is necessary for the development of a granular or crumb structure, which is desirable for growing plants because it allows space between the particles. These minute openings provide space not only for water and for the microscopic roots of plants, but also for air, which is as necessary for the growth of roots as it is for the growth of leaves, stems, and flowers. Many house plants grown in glazed or metal flower pots without drainage die because water fills all the spaces between the soil particles and the roots cannot get air. Roots that are completely submerged may literally drown.

To give weathered rock the properties of soil requires many years or even several lifetimes. Each of the requisites—humus, layering or profile development, and structure—depends on more than the presence of vegetation and millions of insects and microorganisms. The worms and grubs that are visible are very few in number compared with minute bacteria, fungi, and microscopic forms of life. Most of these minute organisms live on the dead remains of plants and actually carry out the decay of old leaves, stems, roots, and other plant parts. The soil, therefore, is not merely broken-up rock. It is a whole world of living things, most too small to be seen. It is a constantly changing layer that loses some of its constituents and gains others. This constant exchange in the soil keeps it in the form most useful to humans—capable of absorbing and holding water and therefore good for growing plants.

Plants take up from the soil not only water but also dissolved mineral material that is necessary for the building of the plant cells. The dissolved materials used by the plants are the soil's mineral nutrients. They are, in a way, the plants' food. With sunlight and water the green leaves of the plant make sugars, which, in turn, are converted to starches and other plant materials.

How much of a plant is made up of the mineral nutrients from the soil? When a log is burned in the fireplace, the amount of remaining ash is very small compared with the original log. The ash contains nearly all the mineral nutrients. The part of the log that went up the chimney as smoke consisted of water and of the organic material manufactured in the leaves. Thus the soil provides only a small but essential part of the plant. It also provides the medium in which the plant can extend its roots and obtain water.

Soil water is absorbed and transpired by plants. This use of water by plants results in soil becoming drier to much greater depths than if the soil were bare and water merely evaporated from the surface. Roots extract most of the available water from the soil in which they are growing. In most areas, plant roots grow to depths of a few meters. In arid parts of the western United States, some roots grow as deep as 15 meters. Evaporation from a bare soil surface will dry the soil to depths ofonl4w4.5yaboutonethirdofameter.

Anyone who has tried to grow shrubbery around the house or a few tomato plants and lettuce in the backyard knows that in the spring the soil is so wet that digging in it is a most unpleasant chore. In late summer, however, the soil is so dry and hard that digging is almost impossible. Again, in autumn, after plants shed their leaves and become dormant, the soil becomes wet. This conspicuous seasonal change in soil moisture is partly the result of the use of water by plants. They use large quantities in summer and almost none in winter.

Besides the seasonal cycle, there is a daily cycle in the use of water. Plants transpire, or lose, most water during a hot, dry, sunny day but lose very little at night. This daily variation in water loss is reflected in the flow of water in small streams draining areas of a few hundred hectares in size. If no rain has fallen for several days, streamflow is highest in the morning hours, reflecting the low rate of water use during the preceding night.

All the water that comes from the atmosphere as precipitation must pass through or over the top layers of the earth, and nearly everywhere this top layer is the soil. Soil erosion and the need to conserve soil are important contemporary problems. Erosion is caused principally by water, and therefore no general discussion of water would be complete without consideration of its relation to the soil-erosion problem.

Some soils take in water more easily than others. In soils with high infiltration rates, little precipitation will run off the surface, and soil loss by erosion will be minimized. Vegetation tends to break the force of the falling raindrops and holds the soil particles together, thus tending to prevent the soil from washing away.

The incorporation of the plant material in the uppermost layer of the soil affects its ability to absorb water. A lush cover of vegetation does not necessarily indicate the presence of large amounts of humus in the soil. The jungles in some tropical countries, for instance, grow on soil that contains very little organic material because of the high rate of decomposition. Once the tropical forest is cut down, rains wash away the soil very quickly because there is nothing to keep the mineral particles from sticking together and, therefore, closing the pores. In contrast, rain can beat down on a bare soil that contains much humus and be rapidly absorbed.

The top layer of the soil erodes first, and this top layer, with its humic material, contains more of the nutrients that are necessary for plants and animals than do the deeper layers. This is because a substantial portion of available soil nutrients are held in the humus, either within the decaying organic matter or as adsorbed materials derived from the organic matter or from the precipitation. Loss of the most fertile topsoil is usually a serious problem because in most areas it cannot be replaced except over long periods of time.

In some areas, the weathered material is deep and bedrock is found at great depth. Under such conditions, even after erosion has removed some meters of the top layers, sufficient material still remains in which plants can grow. The loss of the top layers of a deep soil is less serious than the loss from shallow soil.

Because soils that are protected from erosion by plant cover also absorb water best, soil conservation has frequently been confused with the control of great floods. One view is that floods can be prevented if soils are maintained in their best condition for the rapid infiltration of water. Surface runoff is the principal source of flood water; therefore, water that is absorbed in the soil will not run off. This argument may apply to small or moderate rains but does not apply to great floods.

From a particular rain, a larger percentage of the total water will sink into a well-kept garden patch than will be infiltrated into a fallow field where the soil is bare. The bare soil in Figure 53a is absorbing water less rapidly than the ground surface of Figure 53b; thus, there is more runoff from the bare area. The vegetated plot would, in general, have a greater rate of infiltration and would be comparable to a sieve of large mesh. Corresponding to the fine mesh sieve, the bare soil would absorb some of the rainfall, but most of it would flow to the gutter as surface storm runoff.

In the same rainstorm, all the rain that fell on a roof or an impervious concrete driveway would run off into the gutter, so the gutter would get water as fast as it fell. The first water that infiltrates moistens the soil particles. If there is enough water to moisten the soil all the way down to the water table, any additional water infiltrating can pass downward and add to the amount of water in the saturated zone. The water that moistened the soil particles is retained in the soil and is gradually returned to the atmosphere by evaporation or transpiration during periods of fair weather.

An increase in the infiltration rate caused by changes in the vegetation may, under some circumstances, result in an increase in the amount of water returned to the atmosphere by transpiration and thus

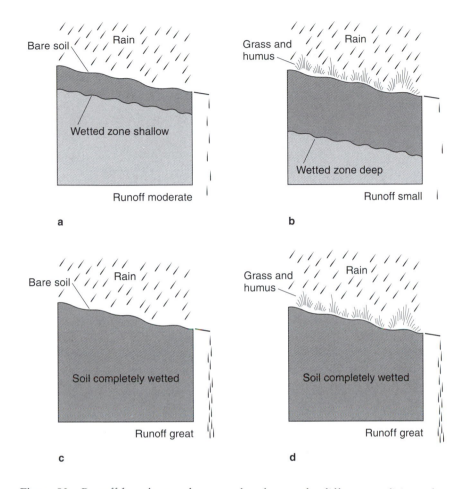

Figure 53 Runoff from bare and vegetated surfaces under different conditions of soil moisture.

reduce the proportion of rain appearing as runoff in surface streams. In areas where there is considerable rainfall, such as the eastern United States, such changes would be relatively trivial because there is a large amount of water available for surface flow. In arid regions, however, increasing the amount of water lost to the atmosphere may appreciably change the amount of runoff in surface streams.

Rainfall enters the soil by infiltration. When there has been enough rain to saturate the soil, the rate of infiltration is greatly decreased and most of the additional rainfall will be rejected and will run off into the streams. Therefore, improvements in vegetation or farming methods intended to increase the infiltration capacity of the surface will be most helpful in deep soils that have a great capacity for receiving and retaining water.

Continued rainfall does two things: It decreases the infiltration rate at the surface and it decreases the capacity of the soil to absorb more water. This is shown in Figures 53c and d, in which both soils are completely wetted. Under this condition the amount of runoff from the grassed areas is approximately the same as from the bare one. When the soil is sufficiently wet, the infiltration rate for bare areas is only slightly different from that of well-vegetated areas; the capacity to receive and retain additional rainfall is essentially the same. Therefore, the amount of vegetation has little effect on the catastrophic flood because such a flood occurs only after a thorough wetting of the soil.

The salts in water

The chemical nature of water is important to humans. Drinking water should not taste salty or of sulfur or iron, but neither should it taste flat like distilled water. It should also be soft enough to lather easily. It is the dissolved chemical compounds called salts that give water its taste and that make it either "hard" or "soft."

The presence of calcium and magnesium compounds make water hard because the calcium and magnesium combine with soap to form insoluble compounds that deposit on skin and in the weave of the cloth being washed. These deposits are extremely difficult to remove, and after continual washing in hard water, white sheets and clothes become the much advertised "tattle-tale gray."

There is great variety of types and quantities of salts in water, and their effects may be vastly different. Table salt, or sodium chloride, which is only one of the many kinds of salts, gives some water a salty taste. Some salts make water hard; yet these same salts can be helpful to irrigation. Others can ruin the soil if used for irrigation; one type can poison crops. One salt, fluoride, that can in high concentration cause mottled teeth, is essential in the protection of teeth from decay.

Rainfall, though not chemically pure, is nearly pure water. As it falls, it is at its purest moment in the entire hydrologic cycle even though it contains dust material washed out of the air, salt carried inland from sea spray, and, most important, carbon dioxide. When rain strikes the ground it immediately comes in contact with many kinds of soluble materials. Most minerals that make up rocks are practically insoluble in water, but over very long periods, appreciable amounts are dissolved. The solvent action of water is increased by the carbon dioxide absorbed from the air. Many chemical elements are taken into solution by the water trickling and flowing through and over the rocks and the soil. Furthermore, new chemical compounds are formed when these elements meet in solution.

Some of the impurities that rain picks up as it falls through the air are simply carried down to earth without being dissolved, and some become dissolved in the water of the rain drops. It is the assimilation of acid materials as rain falls that causes the important problem of acid rain. The U.S. National Academy of Sciences states that the first major cause of acid deposition in the industrialized world is the sulfur dioxide emitted to the atmosphere when coal is burned. The second major source of acidifying compounds is automobiles and power plants that emit nitrogen oxides when fossil fuels are burned.

These oxides are transformed through a variety of chemical reactions into sulfuric and nitric acids. The acids dissolve in water droplets, can be carried long distances, and rain back to earth. Most pure natural waters, including rain and snow, have a pH value of 5.2 to 5.4. A neutral value of pH is 7. All values of pH less than 5 may be considered acidic, and pH 4 is 10 times more acidic than pH 5. But over parts of the northeastern United States the pH of rain is 4.3, sufficiently low to be called acid rain.

Acid precipitation can be neutralized or somewhat buffered while travelling through the soil, before it reaches lakes and streams. However, thin or sandy soils provide very little buffering and result in the delivery of acid water to lakes and streams. Extensive areas of North America and northern Europe are sensitive to acid deposition. The Academy states that in Canada, half of the 700,000 lakes in the six eastern provinces are extremely sensitive to acid deposition. The number of fish species in lakes declines with increasing acidity. Many species are lost at pH values near 6.0. The National Academy lists acid deposition as one of the six most important facets of global environmental change.

The chemistry of water in and on the ground is complex. One source of dissolved matter in water can be illustrated by observing what can happen to one common mineral, feldspar. This is one of the minerals that make up the rock, granite. One kind of feldspar contains oxygen, silicon, aluminum, and sodium. Among these elements sodium is held least tightly to its chemical partners, and so it is removed first in solution. Few elements are dissolved in pure or unattached form; rather, they join with another element or combination of elements to form a new compound. Feldspar is a major source of sodium and silicon in water. Other minerals produce a wide variety of compounds when dissolved in water.

A typical compound, sodium bicarbonate, is formed by the bonding of sodium to some of the carbon dioxide that the rainwater picks up while passing through the atmosphere. Groundwater commonly contains carbon dioxide and could therefore be called a weak carbonated water. The fizz in a carbonated drink is made up of dissolved carbon dioxide.

Some rocks are more soluble than others. Lava is relatively insoluble. Limestone and gypsum are very soluble; when they are exposed to flowing water, they dissolve and become a source of calcium, carbonate, and sulfate. Solution of limestone forms caves. Carlsbad Caverns in New Mexico and Mammoth Cave in Kentucky are examples of the fantastic shape and size of underground tunnels that may result from dissolution.

The quantity of mineral matter carried by water depends chiefly on the type of rocks and soils with which the water comes in contact, but the length of time of the contact is also important. Groundwater usually contains more dissolved mineral matter than surface water because groundwater remains in contact with rocks and soils for longer periods. Most streams are fed by both surface water and groundwater. During dry periods, river waters therefore generally reflect the chemical character of groundwater. Because river waters carry less dissolved material during rainy periods or when there is heavy snowmelt, river water varies more in chemical character than groundwater.

As previously mentioned, rainwater is almost pure. It usually contains less than 10 parts per million of dissolved matter; that is, 1 million kilograms of water contains 10 kilograms of dissolved material. Dissolved materials increase steadily in quantity as the water flows through the hydrologic cycle and reaches a maximum in basins such as the oceans, from which distilled water is returned to the air via evaporation.

The dissolved material in rivers is usually less than 500 parts per million but some rivers may contain 2,000 or more parts per million. A total dissolved solid concentration of more than 500 parts per million or one half gram per liter is considered undesirable for the public water supply of a city. Many nations specify acceptable concentrations of each major contaminant separately rather than as a single TDS value.

Some groundwater, called brine, contains more than 10,000 parts per million of salt and is much too salty for most uses. Sea water contains 35,000 parts per million (3.5 percent) of salt. At low stage, Utah's Great Salt Lake is nearly saturated and contains approximately 250,000 parts per million (25 percent) of common salt; this means that a liter of lake water contains 250 grams of salt in solution.

As water is heated to the boiling point, the dissolved salts do not leave with the vapor but are left in the pan. They tend to deposit on the walls of the container in which the water is heated. Heat tends to drive off some of the carbon dioxide gas that had helped dissolve the material from the rocks through which water passed. When the carbon dioxide is driven off, the material derived from the rocks precipitates. Salt deposits can be found in tea kettles, hot water tanks in homes, and boilers in industrial plants. The coating, or "scale," is similar to limestone. When deposited on the walls of a tank or boiler, it not only takes up space but adds markedly to fuel costs. A coating 3 mm thick increases fuel use by 10 percent.

Sodium is an element that causes trouble on irrigated farms. Sodium salts tend to make a soil sticky when wet and to form clods when dry, with the results that plants absorb water only with difficulty. It also has harmful effects on plant growth. Calcium, which makes water hard and thus less desirable in homes and factories, generally is beneficial in irrigation farming, for it tends to make the soil crumb-like and thus ideal for plant root growth and water absorption. Boron is one of several mineral constituents needed in very small quantities for plant growth. In large amounts, however, boron is poisonous to plants.

Chemically pure water has a flat taste; for this reason people prize the "flavor" of water from springs and wells. This water contains small but significant amounts of salts in solution. Salts in natural waters may be harmful or beneficial, so it is important to know the amount and kind of salts in the water supply and how they affect the potential use of the water.

The total mass of dissolved material in surface water is surprisingly large. World surface water has a dissolved load between 32 and 37 metric tons per square kilometer per year (90 to 104 tons per square mile per year). Rivers in arid climates carry more sediment and a smaller proportion of dissolved material than rivers in more humid regions. The ratio of solid to dissolved load is 46 for the Colorado River of the United States and 10.5 for the Brahmaputra. Low values of the ratio include 0.3 for the Ob, 1.7 for the Amazon, 6.9 for the Ganges, and 1.1 for the Congo.

II

The Water Resource and Its Management

Water Supply

If the flows of all the largest rivers in the world are totalled, the addition of successively smaller rivers makes less and less difference. The majority of the water flowing to the oceans is carried by a few very large rivers, and all the water flowing in all the creeks, runs, branches and streams added together are but a small part of the total.

There are 1.3 billion cubic kilometers of water on earth. The oceans contain 97% of that volume. Compared with this figure, the quantity of water in all other locations is small. This fact is emphasized in Table 1, which shows that the freshwater portion is only a small percentage. The seas are salty and therefore of limited use for water supply. An appreciable part of the world's water, two percent, is frozen in the icecaps and glaciers.

The Antarctic icecap covers 15 million square kilometers and contains 85 percent of the frozen water. If this icecap were melted at a uniform rate, the melt water would feed the Mississippi for 50,000 years, or it would feed all the rivers in the United States for 17,000 years.

The water vapor in the atmosphere is derived from evaporation from oceans and land and from transpiration from plants. Approximately 389,000 cubic kilometers of water goes into the air annually as water vapor. Of this amount, 328,000 cubic kilometers are evaporated from the world's oceans. 291,000 cubic kilometers of evaporated water fall back to the oceans and 37,000 cubic kilometers fall on land and feed rivers and springs. The remaining 61,000 cubic kilometers infiltrate into the land surface and are available for absorption by plants and replenishment of ground storage.

Table 1
Water on the earth

Location	Water volume (cubic km)	Percentage of total water
SURFACE WATER		
Fresh-water lakes	123,000	.009
Saline lakes and inland seas	102,000	.008
Average in stream channels	1,229	.0001
SUBSURFACE WATER		
Water in unsaturated aerated zone (includes soil moisture)	65,500	.005
Groundwater within depth of ½ mile	4,100,000	.31
Groundwater, deep lying	4,100,000	.31
OTHER WATER LOCATIONS		
Icecaps and glaciers	28,700,000	2.15
Atmosphere (at sea level)	12,700	.001
World ocean	1.3 billion	97.2
Totals (rounded)	**1.335 billion**	100

Engelmann et al. (for Population Action International) provide the following summary of the earth's water:

- Total water on earth, 1.4 billion cubic kilometers (835 million cubic miles), enough to cover the United States to a depth of 150 km or 150,000 m.

- Total renewable water provided by precipitation on continents and islands each year: 41,000 cubic kilometers (10,000 cubic miles), enough to cover the United states to a depth of 4.4 meters.

The water budget

When a hydrologist or student of water studies the water supplies of an area, one of the first things he/she does is to set up a water budget—a

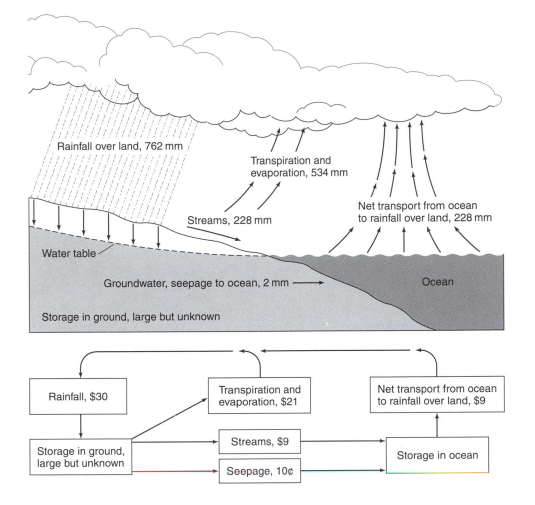

Figure 54 Water budget of the continental United States.

balance sheet—of the receipts, disbursements, and on-hand supplies of water. Existing information about water is rather spotty, and this makes it difficult to prepare a detailed day-to-day water budget for watersheds serving towns or cities with water. However, average annual totals are sufficient to estimate an annual budget for the United States as a whole.

The occurrence of water in the atmosphere, on and in the ground, and in the oceans is summarized in Figure 54, which shows the water cycle and the items to be listed in the budget. Arrows directed toward the land surface designate the input or credit items in the budget.

131

Those leading from the land indicate output or debit items. The quantities could be expressed in various ways, such as liters or cubic meters, but they are more easily understood when expressed in terms of centimeters or millimeters of depth over the United States. Accordingly, 1 cm of water would be equivalent to the amount of water required to cover the country 1 cm deep. One centimeter over the United States would be equivalent to 198 cubic kilometers or 5.5 times the storage capacity of Lake Mead behind Hoover Dam, one of the largest reservoirs in the country.

As mentioned above, in Figure 54, the inputs of water may be considered credit items; amounts of water withdrawn or depleted represent debit items:

• *Credit:* The input is entirely in the form of rainfall and snowfall. This precipitation averages approximately 762 mm over the United States each year.

• *Debit:* The removal of water from the land includes the flow of streams, deep seepage of groundwater to the oceans, transpiration from plants, and evaporation from lakes, ponds, swamps, rivers, and soil.

The annual discharge of rivers to the sea amounts to 228 mm. It is interesting to note that of this amount, 40 percent is carried by the Mississippi River alone. The amount of deep seepage from groundwater to the sea is not known, but is believed to be quite small, probably much less than 2.5 mm per year. Evaporation from wet surfaces and transpiration from plants are similar processes which, when combined is the evapotranspiration. The total over the United States averages approximately 534 mm per year.

An examination of these figures reveals that for the land area of the continent, the water cycle balances as follows: credit, 762 mm from precipitation; debit, 228 mm runoff of rivers plus 534 mm evaporated and transpired. However, if the atmosphere is examined, the cycle appears out of balance because the atmosphere delivers 762 mm to the land as rain and snow but receives only 534 mm from evapotranspiration. The atmosphere makes up this difference of 228 mm by transporting moisture from the oceans to the continent to balance the discharge of rivers to the sea.

The atmospheric moisture budget balances each year, but not much is known about the capital stock, that is, the amount in the lakes, groundwater, and soil. The stock of water on hand is relatively stable.

Most measurements have attempted to determine how the water stocks in different places change from season to season or from year to year rather than estimate the total amount. For example, it has been estimated that there is an average seasonal change in soil moisture of 100 mm per year in the eastern part of the United States. The seasonal range in groundwater storage in the eastern part of the country is approximately the same. Changes in soil moisture plus groundwater add up to approximately 200 mm during the course of a year. Thus seasonal fluctuation of water on hand is not very large. This seasonal variation is quite distinct from the total amount of water in the ground and in the soil. The total amount is very large, but available data are so meager that a meaningful estimate is quite impossible.

The fluctuating water supply

Weather changes from day to day but climate changes as well, both in the long term and in periods of less than a century. Much of North America, as far south as New York City and St. Louis, was once covered by glacial ice. The weather was obviously colder and wetter than it is today. Desert areas in California, Nevada, and Utah were not deserts then, and many small and large lakes existed in places where the weather is now dry enough for horned toads and sagebrush. A computation of the climate needed to maintain a lake in what is now semi-arid New Mexico indicates that the temperature in summer was 3.3° C lower than the present and the annual precipitation was 230 mm higher. California's Death Valley was once a lake; Utah's Great Salt Lake is a remnant of Lake Bonneville that once covered 49,000 sq km.

The last major glacial phase ended approximately 12,000 years ago. Since the ice melted, the climate has changed several times. Somewhere between 5,000 and 8,000 years ago the continent was warmer and drier than it is today, a period called the Altithermal. Temperatures were so high that most of the mountain glaciers in North America and Europe disappeared completely. Some Europeans refer to this period as the Climatic Optimum.

A relatively cool period followed and was interrupted, at least in the southwestern states, by an extended drought that appears to have lasted from about 1200 to 1400 AD. This period of relative warmth probably permitted the Vikings to settle in Greenland about 1000 AD and reconnoiter along the northern coast of North America.

In Europe, the Middle Ages were cold and stormy. Even in recent times there was a cold and wet period. The mountain glaciers of western North America probably reached their maximum size in the late nineteenth century. At that time glaciers were larger than at present, and so the period is called the Little Ice Age, but for the past few decades the glaciers have been shrinking by melting. The climate during the first half of the twentieth century has shown a warming trend, in comparison with the period of 1870–1900. In the 1950s, the warming trend began to slow, and some mountain glaciers again began to reach a little farther down their valleys. The variability of weather and record-breaking observations in the last decades of the twentieth century are considered by many to be the precursors of a world-wide warming associated with changes in the composition of the earth's atmosphere due to human use of resources. The 1994–95 World Resources Institute report presents a brief but broad review of the data of recent global warming and the degree of consensus within the scientific community on various warming issues.

Climatic changes through geologic time must have been very sharply marked and have lasted many centuries. The earliest records must be read in the rocks. Fossil plants and animals are a clue to the climate of their time. The deposits of sand and gravel in moraines, scour marks in hard rocks, and U-shaped valleys are evidence of glaciation. The bones of arctic animals far south of their present habitat are also evidence of glacial cold.

When humans appeared on the earth, they made tools and clothing that tell a story about the climate of the time. After learning to write, approximately 50 centuries ago, they wrote about crops and left records that tell a more precise story. The development of science and scientific instruments have made possible the recording of rainfall and temperature and thus the direct measurement of climate. Some climate records go back 200 years. The longest record in the United States, that of the temperatures in New Haven, Connecticut, was begun about 1750, and was at first kept by physicians and clergymen who made the observations as a matter of personal interest and curiosity. The rainfall record at Santa Fe, New Mexico, was begun in 1849. It was originally kept by the physician at the Army post. This record is short compared with the 2,000 years of observation of the stages of the Nile or the 1,000 years of record of some river gages in China. There are also ancient rainfall records in China.

Because fresh water is derived from rainfall, water supplies are linked to the weather. Weather and streamflow are variable. Over the long run a given location will experience a pattern of wet and dry, hot and cold weather. But the pattern is not necessarily repetitive. The thousands of cities, irrigators, and power-plant operators that obtain their water supply from streams all wish to know as much as possible about present and future fluctuations in flow. Measurements of river flows constitute streamflow records, which can be used to predict streamflow for short periods in advance. The principal considerations used in preparing a forecast are as follows.

Streamflow is derived from rainfall or snowmelt; the greater the amount of precipitation, the greater the streamflow. But infiltration into the soil has first call on available rainwater or snowmelt; the drier the soil, the greater the amount of water retained by it. These two factors, the amount of precipitation and the state of soil moisture, determine the amount of runoff. To make a forecast, therefore, the hydrologist measures the precipitation and deducts from it the amount of water that will be retained by the soil. The difference between precipitation and retention is an estimate of the runoff.

The forecast can also be made once the precipitation has fallen on the ground. With the measurement of precipitation available, streamflow applies only to the precipitation that is measured. Streamflow resulting from a rainstorm may be forecast only over the few hours or days that are required for a river to rise and subside. This is called flood forecasting. Forecasts of streamflow from the melting of a winter's accumulation of snow in the high mountains of the western United States may be made two to four months in advance. The snow reaches its maximum accumulation at the end of March. The melting does not occur until late spring or early summer. Thus snow surveys made in the early spring can give forecasts of the runoff over the warm months ahead.

Streamflow is what is left over after precipitation has supplied the demands of vegetation and the process of evaporation. Leftovers or differences tend to vary greatly with time. For example, suppose that the rainfall in one year is 100 cm and that evaporation and plant transpiration 50 cm. This leaves 50 cm to be carried off by the streams. Suppose that in the next year rainfall is 75 cm, 25 percent less than in the previous year. If evaporation and transpiration were the same, which is quite possible, streamflow would be only 25 cm, 50 percent less than in the year before. Thus a 25 percent change in rainfall becomes a 50 percent change in runoff. This means that the flow of streams is highly variable and sensitive to changes in rainfall.

River discharge in the United States is characterized by the high flows in the earlier parts of the records. There is a discernible downward trend in flow volume that is most marked in western streams.

During the period of record, the period of lowest streamflow in the United States occurred during the decade 1930–1940, with a fortunate upswing during the war years when there were rapidly mounting demands for water. In the late 1960s a downward trend again appeared.

Ever since record collection began, hydrologists have plotted graphs and wondered whether the ups and downs represent cyclic changes. For some rivers, the record appears to be repetitive or cyclic. There are many cyclic changes in nature, and nearly all are related to the day or year, day and night, and the four seasons of the year. The tides too are cyclic, and indeed daily tides are forecast years in advance.

Despite the success in forecasting tides, very little success has come from efforts to extend the apparent cycles in the long records of streamflow. At present it is known merely that these ups and downs are part of the pattern of streamflow and that variations as great or even greater than those of the past can be expected. The downward trend, except as affected by uses of water and land, is not likely to persist indefinitely, but just when and in what manner changes will occur cannot be foretold. Tomorrow's weather can be forecast reasonably well; less accurate but useful forecasts of weather can be made 5 days ahead, and speculations can be made of the weather 30 days ahead. Long-term forecasts of weather or of streamflow are not yet possible.

The long term future is judged by comparison with the past. Streamflow for the coming year cannot be accurately forecast, but past records can be used to predict the probability, for example, of a flood of any given height. Suppose that in the past 100 years, a given river reached a height of 10 meters 5 times, or an average of once every 20 years. It might then be expected that in the next 100 years, the river will also reach the 10 meter stage 5 times; however when these 5 floods will come cannot be predicted. They could all come within a single 20-year period.

An actual view of variability can be obtained by analyzing the yearly flows in the Columbia River. In the 90-year record of the river (a rather long period as records go), yearly average flows have varied greatly. The greatest annual flow was 2.2 times the lowest annual flow. The averages of 10-year periods have also varied, but less, the greatest being 1.45 times the least. For 20-year periods the highest average was 1.3 times the lowest. Thus variability decreases as the length of the period increases, but variability never becomes zero. It is known that considerable variability remains between periods even as long as 200 years. When using streamflow records, allowance must be made for this variability; that is, the possibility that the flow will be even more or even less than any previously experienced flow.

The water user is in a dilemma. If he limits his use to only a small part of the available water in order to ensure supply, then water goes by unused. If he uses too much of the available water, the risk of shortage becomes great. As a consequence of the variable nature of streamflow, every nation faces this problem. Because of variability of flow, all the water can never be put to use.

Water Use

Water that goes into ground storage or surface runoff is the total supply available for human demands. The rest is lost to the atmosphere. This total supply varies enormously from one country to another. The 1990 annual renewable freshwater available per person was computed for the 100 countries with the least supply by Population Action International. The figures vary from 75 cubic meters per year per person in Kuwait to 13,400 in Luxembourg. The figures for the United States were 14,900 cubic meters in 1955 and 9,900 in 1990. The available supply in most countries decreased in that 35-year period due to population increase. It is generally agreed that 1000 cubic meters per person per year represents water scarcity. Canada's supply is over 100,000 cubic meters per person.

Available fresh water is not necessarily equal to the amount withdrawn. The latter depends on the development of infrastructure. Data on water withdrawals and its uses for most countries of the world have been compiled in the publication entitled *World Resources*.

In any discussion of the uses of water, it must be remembered that some uses result in actual consumption or loss of water to the atmosphere as vapor. For example, a gardener tries to sprinkle water near the plant roots. Because water taken up by the plant is transpired to the atmosphere as vapor, the water is unavailable for further use by man. Irrigation, therefore, is a consumptive use of water. In contrast, water used for such normal household purposes as bathing, dishwashing, and toilet flushing is not consumed but is mostly returned to the surface streams via the municipal sewer system. For this reason, such household uses are nonconsumptive uses.

Use of water in the home

Water is used in the home for drinking, cooking, washing clothes and dishes, but the purposes using the largest amounts are bathing, toilet flushing, and lawn sprinkling. Together these are called domestic uses. The average daily use per person in an American home varies between 200 and 500 liters. Listed below are some typical quantities of water necessary for certain home operations.

- Flush a toilet   11 liters
- Take a bath   115 to 150 liters
- Take a shower   75 to 115 liters
- Wash dishes   40 liters
- Operate a washing machine   75 to 115 liters

It is estimated that the average family use of water in the United States is as follows in liters per day per person:

- Lawn irrigation   95
- Toilets   91
- Bathing   75
- Laundry   53
- Dishes   16
- Drinking and cooking   8

Ordinary customs in daily life can result in needless water use and a little consideration can save an appreciable amount of the resource. If a man lets the water run in the sink while shaving, he wastes about 85 liters. If the tap runs while he brushes his teeth, the loss can be about 42 liters.

Water use in the author's home will furnish a specific example.

In Berkeley, California, the author's family used 380 liters per day per person in the rainy season. The amount increased to 800 liters per person per day in summer when the garden was watered. The average charge for water in Berkeley is 53 cents per thousand liters, so we paid about 20 cents per day per person in winter. This is about the average cost in cities of the United States.

Waste of water in the home can increase the bill by several dollars.

A dripping faucet that leaks only one drop each second will waste 15 liters a day. A leak into a toilet bowl, which is not seen but detected only as an unimportant hum in the pipe, may easily amount to 6 liters per hour. This would be a waste of 52,000 liters per year.

A charge of 53 cents per thousand kilograms results in a ton of water delivered at the tap. Thus water is, as the saying goes, cheap as dirt. In fact, water is much cheaper than dirt. Delivery of a ton of dirt would cost several thousand dollars.

It must be emphasized that in the United States the consumer is not paying the true cost of supplying the water because there are subsidies. So, the figures above do not reflect the true cost to the government and to society. If the consumer were charged the true cost of water, greater efforts would be made to conserve.

Use of water in the cities

In many cities each home has a water meter to measure water use, and the consumer pays for just what he takes. Elsewhere a person pays a flat rate regardless of how much he uses. Water engineers have found that families are much more economical in the use of water when their use is individually measured by a meter. Families paying a flat rate use, on the average, twice as much water as those whose use is metered.

Water use varies during the day and during the week in a way that reflects some interesting details of American home life. Use is, of course, low during the night but increases rapidly to a maximum between 8 and 9 o'clock in the morning. Another peak occurs between 6 and 8 o'clock in the evening. Though there is variation in maximum peak between cities, this difference is interpreted to mean that more people shower in the morning than at bedtime. Also, an extra heavy peak occurs on Saturday night in many cities; so it appears that the Saturday night bath or shower is still a reality.

Though water use in the home is usually thought of as the principal reason for the existence of a municipal system, industries are also major users of water from municipal systems. Many industrial plants find it more economical to buy water from the city than to provide individual supplies from wells or reservoirs. Average use by commerce and industry is approximately 265 liters per capita per day.

In addition to domestic and industrial uses, there are two other main classes of water use in municipal supplies: public use, which includes fire extinguishing, street cleaning, public-building use, and maintenance of public parks, and which accounts for an additional 30 liters per capita per day. Loss or unaccounted-for waste is large. Leaks from water mains and unmeasured leaks from faucets, as well as errors of measurement, contribute to this loss. Generally, even careful construction and management cannot reduce water loss to less than 20 percent of the total use.

In total, the average use of water per capita in American cities has risen progressively with the increase in productive activity. But 50 percent of the municipal water use in summer was to irrigate lawns and fill swimming pools. In 1920 the average use was only 435 liters per day per capita. The record shows that there was a 50 percent increase in 40 years.

Though many industries buy water from the public or municipal supply system, it is common for large factories to put in their own wells or surface reservoirs. The latter type of industrial use may be classified as self-supplied. Statistics on amounts of water for municipal use include the amount of water purchased by some industries.

Annual use

The World Resources Institute estimates that 69 percent of worldwide water use is for agriculture. It estimates that the global renewable water resource is 7,420 cubic meters per capita per year, but that many countries have far more limited supplies. In Egypt, for example, the per capita renewable amount is 50 cubic meters, far below the country's withdrawal of 1,028 cubic meters per year. Canada has a supply of over 100,000 cubic meters per capita. A tabulation of the annual renewable fresh water for the world, country by country, is presented by Population Action International in the publication *Sustaining Water*.

The total water-use figure in the United States of 910,000 million liters per day amounts to approximately one-fifth of the amount available for use. It can be said, then, that at present Americans are using only 1 liter out of every 5 available. Of each liter now being used, only 7 percent is used for public water supplies. The remaining percentage is divided equally between irrigation and industry. These figures indicate that there is no overall shortage of water in the United States; however, the uneven distribution engenders many problems.

An adequate water supply does not prevent the occurrence of local shortages and excesses, which result from the irregular distribution of precipitation among the arid Southwest, the humid East, and the very rainy mountains of the Northwest. Similar types of problems arise from the season-to-season and year-to-year variation of precipitation in any given area and from the chance occurrence of series of dry years.

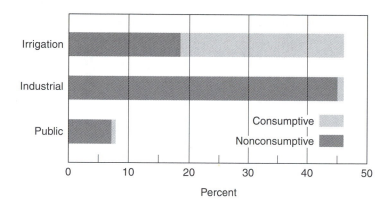

Figure 55 Water use in the United States. Of the 46 percent used for irrigation, 60 percent is consumptive use. Neither industrial nor public use results in such large consumptive losses.

Some of these facts can be summarized in diagrammatic form. Figure 55 shows the division of water withdrawn or used for public and industrial uses and for irrigation use in the United States. The part of each that is lost by consumptive use is indicated in the diagrams. The consumptive use of water amounts to about 36 percent of all use and nearly all of that is in irrigation. Industry uses water primarily for cooling and although the total use is large, nearly all of it is returned to streams, lakes or the ground. However, the water returned is somewhat degraded in quality, mostly by the heat it contains.

Figure 56 shows the sources of water. Most of it is withdrawn from lakes and streams; 20 percent is withdrawn from groundwater. Saline water represents approximately 10 percent of the water used; all the rest is fresh water.

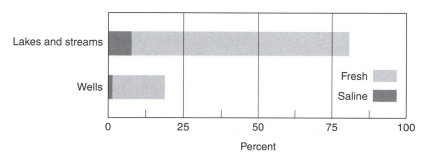

Figure 56 Source and character of water withdrawn for all uses. Eighty percent of the water used is from lakes and streams and 20 percent is from ground sources.

To appreciate the resource flow in cities, Figure 57 indicates the material taken in and exported from a city of 1 million persons. The figures are given in units of tons per day. It can be seen that the largest item of both import and export is water: The import is in the form of fresh water for city uses, and the export is in the form of sewage. Food brought into the city is only one third of 1 percent of the tonnage represented by water. Other than water as sewage, the largest item of export from the city is refuse, and the second largest is carbon monoxide. Most of the latter is carried away in the atmosphere.

Irrigation

Plants, like people, need a regular supply of water. Of course, some plants require much more water than others. Many of the grasses and some of the cereals, including wheat and barley, do not use as much water as alfalfa, for example. Because the plants that are the most important sources of food and fiber require relatively large amounts of water, most agricultural areas of the United States receive at least 500 to 750 mm of precipitation a year.

If crops are to be grown in areas that do not receive enough rainfall during the growing season, the land must be supplied with extra water. Some places have more than enough rainfall in a year to grow any crop, but the rains are inadequate during the growing season. The result is short-term droughts, and during such periods many farmers find it profitable to irrigate their high-priced crops to maintain a high yield and/or a high product quality.

There are approximately 12 million hectares of irrigated land in the United States. Most of them lie in the 17 western states. In 1950 less than 0.8 million hectares of land were being irrigated in the remaining states. More than 1/4 of the total irrigated area is in California, more than 1/8 is in Texas, and approximately 1/10 is in Colorado and Idaho each.

Worldwide, irrigation has become increasingly important to provide food for growing populations. Since 1955, the amount of land being irrigated has tripled. The World Resources Institute estimates that of the agricultural land currently irrigated, 200 million hectares are in developing countries. In 1990, 270 million hectares of land worldwide were irrigated, supplying a third of the world's harvested crops. Agriculture is the primary use of water for two thirds of the countries of the world. The area of irrigated land worldwide doubled in the first half of

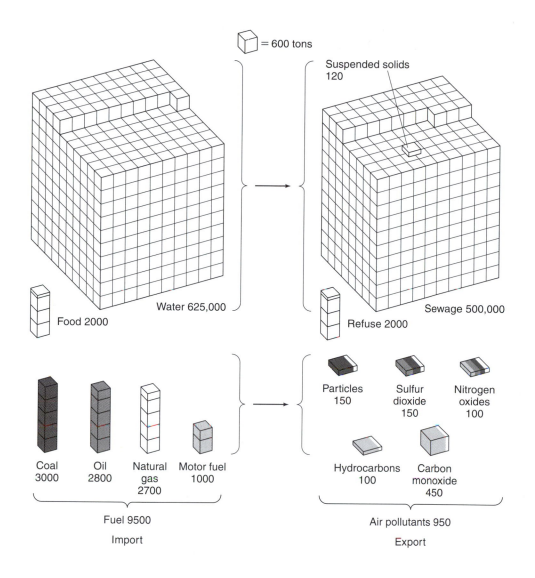

Figure 57 Input and outflow from a modern city of 1 million persons. The flow of materials is expressed as tons per day. Water is the major item.

the twentieth century. It doubled again between 1950 and 1990. In the United States, 13 percent of the cropland is irrigated, but this land produces one third of the value of crops produced.

In the more humid parts of the United States, irrigation increased rapidly in the 1950s, especially in the eastern states, but in the last decade the irrigated area has decreased slightly as urbanization has taken up land formerly farmed. Though the bulk of the irrigated land occupies only a portion of the drier parts of the country, approximately 46 percent of all the water used in the United States is for irrigation. One of the reasons that irrigation is the major use of water is that the cost of water is heavily subsidized by all levels of government. The actual cost of water is on the order of ten to 20 times the amount actually charged to an irrigator.

Irrigation is a consumptive use; that is, most of the water is transpired or evaporated to the atmosphere and is lost to further use by man. Irrigation accounts for the largest portion of the water removed, but not returned, from the stream systems.

Irrigation demands are large, as are the units needed to describe them. In the United States, acre-feet are used, rather than gallons. An acre-foot is the quantity of water that will cover 1 acre of land 1 foot deep and is equivalent to 326,000 gallons or 1,236 cu m. A stream of water delivering 1 cubic foot per second, or 7.5 gallons per second, will yield 2 acre-feet in a day's time. Even in agriculture the expression of water volume is switching from acre feet to cubic meters.

The amount of water required to raise a crop depends on the kind of crop and the climate. The most important climatic characteristic governing water need is the length of the growing season. Since growing seasons are longer in the southern United States, the volume of water required for growth is larger there. Because the growing season is shorter in the cool mountains than in the warmer plains, water requirements decrease at higher elevations.

The following examples give an idea of the amount of water necessary to grow some of the common crops. The quantities are expressed in centimeters of water necessary to grow the crop in an area where the growing season is approximately 200 days, the average for places where irrigation is widely practiced. Alfalfa requires approximately 89 cm of water; sugar beets need 76 cm; cotton, 63 cm; and potatoes, 51 cm. The water requirement can be supplied by rain during the growing season or by irrigation when adequate water is not supplied by rainfall.

If the transport of water from the stream to the field were efficient, irrigation would use much less water than it does currently. Under current practices, considerable waste occurs. Many irrigation canals and ditches through which the water flows are not lined with concrete or other water-tight material but are merely excavated in the earth. Water flowing in such a ditch tends to seep into the ground, and thus a considerable amount is lost on its way to the farm. Some excess water leaves the irrigated field, so the growing crop does not get to use all the water that the farmer applies to the field. The loss is usually 35 to 50 percent of the total taken out of the stream.

However, not all of the water lost from ditches or wasted on the field is completely unavailable for man's use. Much of the water that seeps into the ground moves toward a stream channel and reappears as water flowing in a river. In addition, some of the water that flows off the irrigated field is picked up by a drainage ditch and eventually is returned to some surface stream, where it is again available for possible use. As a consequence of these losses, much more water must be taken from the stream than the previously mentioned figures would indicate.

As an example of the amount of water used in irrigation, a group of irrigated farms served by a single main canal in southern Arizona might include 8,000 hectares of irrigated land. This project would require approximately 135 million cubic meters of water per year. Of this amount, 90 million cubic meters, or two thirds, would be transpired by plants to the atmosphere and would thus be lost to further use by man. Such an amount would support a city of approximately 500,000 people. The remaining 44 million cubic meters "wasted" in the transportation of water is still part of the regional resource because some of the "waste" returns to the stream from which it was diverted.

Irrigation is more complex than it might appear at first glance. Applying water to the land is an art, and experience is necessary to do the job well. If too little water is applied to a field, the dissolved salts accumulate in the soil just as white lime accumulates in a tea kettle as water continually boils away. Salinization of soil is a worldwide problem. In the Plan Blue for the Mediterranean, Michel Batisse estimates that, due to irrigation in the Nile Valley, 30 percent of the soil is salinized and 40 percent is showing signs of becoming so.

If enough water is applied to the field so that a considerable amount sinks into the soil in excess of that needed by plants, this excess water tends to carry the salts down to the water table where they are beyond the reach of plant roots. Accumulation of salts in the soil is undesirable, as mentioned previously, because, when in excess, they tend to make the soil sticky when wet and hard and cloddy when dry. A means of disposal of this surplus soil water is necessary. Otherwise this water, added to the groundwater, raises the water table. If drainage is not provided, the land will become waterlogged. Practically all irrigated areas have drainage problems. But irrigation leads to an increase of salt loading of water that returns to the river from drainage ditches.

Because of salt leaching and drainage the amount of water applied to the field must be carefully chosen. The rate of water application is also important. If the water is applied too fast, the soil cannot absorb the water; consequently, much runs off the surface and is wasted. Fields that were not adequately smoothed collect too much water in the low spots and are insufficiently watered on the mounds. To achieve uniform crops over the whole field requires careful soil preparation. Some of this preparation is avoided by use of the recently developed system of sprinkler irrigation, which results in improved water distribution.

Large fields can be sprinkler irrigated by immense sprinkler heads and lightweight, mobile metal pipes. In many areas, fields are sprinkled from large nozzles mounted on permanent standpipes; the main distributing pipes are buried underground, out of the reach of plows and tillage equipment. Obviously, these sprinkler systems are more expensive than the older and more universal systems of furrow or flooding irrigation from an open ditch.

The drip irrigation system developed in Israel is now in wide use. Water is delivered to individual plants drop by drop. This method has the immense advantage of efficient and direct delivery of water to the plant root. It reduces the potential for salinization of soil and eliminates much of the need for drainage ditches.

It can be seen, then, that farming under irrigation is more complex than merely applying water to compensate for a deficiency in rainfall. The farmer who irrigates must not only pay for the cost of his irrigation system and the extra labor necessary to operate it, but he must also fertilize and spray properly, expensive operations that are profitable only when there is a generous yield of high-priced crops. Irrigation farming therefore requires more time and effort of farm management than does ordinary farming. Not every farmer has the money to start an irrigated farm, the training to operate it, or the desire to expend the necessary effort required for success.

As stated earlier, irrigated agriculture produces about one third of the harvested crops in the world. It is an important contributor to the lives and economics of the world peoples. But irrigation has several drawbacks.

Irrigation consumptively uses more water than any other activity, and this use is increasingly in direct competition with other needs for water. In southern Arizona, costs of water have risen due to lowering of the groundwater level, thus increasing pumping costs. To offset this growing scarcity of groundwater, an expensive canal of large size was constructed to carry water from the Colorado River into the irrigated land in the Salt River Basin. But the imported water is very expensive and of marginal quality because it was drawn from downstream reaches of the river, below a whole series of irrigation projects that increase the salt concentration of the river.

As a result of these circumstances agriculture in central Arizona has diminished and urbanization encroaches on some of the most fertile land. The Arizona situation appears to be gradually settled as the irrigated area is reduced and urban expansion claims the water. But in California, the struggle has not reached a climax. Water is pumped in large volume from the Sacramento River, led in large canals to agriculture in the Central Valley and to cities in southern California. But reduction of fresh water flow into the great estuary of San Francisco Bay is associated with decimation of various species of fish and degradation of other environmental values. In this case, the conflicting uses are irrigated agriculture, urban needs, and fish, wildlife and the environment. The regulated outflow from the Delta to San Francisco Bay is 35 to 50 percent less than pre-diversion outflow. As a result, the number of years considered critically dry is double the number occurring under natural conditions.

The quality of water in rivers providing water for irrigation is decreased by the salt leached from irrigated land and discharged to the river. An example is the change downstream of salt loading in the Colorado River system in western United States. Salinity concentration in the river is influenced by geology and by urban use, but these effects are considered small compared with those of the irrigated districts distributed along the river length. A major tributary of the Colorado River is the Green River that heads in the Wind River Range of western Wyoming. One of the headwater streams, Pine Creek, comes out of the extensively studied glacial Fremont Lake. This lake's water is so pure that it ranks as the second most pure in the United States. It has less than 18 mg/l of dissolved solids. About 130 miles downstream below the Flaming Gorge Reservoir, the total dissolved solids water in the Green River may reach 500 mg/l, but most users experience a level of 350 mg/l. When the river reaches Boulder Dam in Arizona, the concentration is 700 mg/l and farther downstream at Imperial Dam, it is 800 mg/l.

A third problem related to irrigation is the construction of dams.

Until the middle of the twentieth century, there was a general and complacent feeling among both professionals and the public that dams on rivers were a benign alternative to burning fossil fuels. Hydropower generation was considered pollution-free. So widespread was irrigation that to provide the water, reservoir storage was essential not only for water supply but for smoothing out the natural highs and lows of water flows. Added to those apparently desirable results was the concept of multi-purpose dams built to simultaneously provide flood control, irrigation water, and hydropower.

Some of the adverse effects of dams have surfaced in recent decades. In the United States the decimation of salmon fisheries has brought the public to look more closely at side effects of river control by dams. In the same decades, recreation, especially water recreation, has become important to people and also to big business.

Water Availability and Its Quality

Safe drinking water; relation to population

There seems to be no dissent from the conclusion that in the future, availability of water will be as important as ethnic strife or religious difference as the cause of political and social unrest or conflict. Particularly in those regions of the world that are semi-arid or arid, water is an issue. For an accommodation between Israel and the Palestinians, the division of the limited water supply will be of immense importance. And of course, Jordan and Lebanon also have a stake in any such division. Similarly, the fact that Turkey is located at a headwater position above Iraq is also important. In the central part of the African continent, the problem is less the volume of water than it is its availability and quality. Some 80 countries with 40 percent of the world's population suffer from water shortages at some time during a year.

Population Action International reviewed the work of several scholars who have studied the mimimum requirement for maintaining health. They conclude that there is a necessity threshold of about 1,700 cubic meters per year per person. When the renewable supply falls below 1,000 cubic meters per year per person, there is a chronic water scarcity.

The lack of water for irrigation is not as severe a problem as the deficiency of water for drinking and sanitation. The same studies showed that in 1980, 1.8 billion people lacked access to clean drinking water and 1.7 billion lacked adequate sanitation services. Unfortunately, despite real progress toward increasing availability, the simultaneous increase in population overpowers the advancement of facilities. This

151

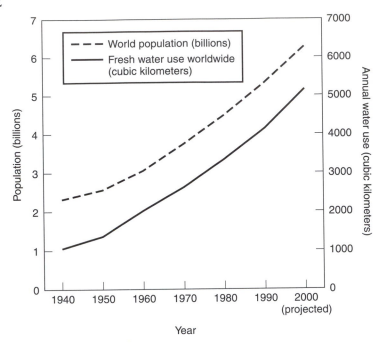

Figure 58 Since 1940, fresh water used by humans has quadrupled as world population has doubled. (Adapted from Population Action International, 1993).

can be seen in Figure 58 that shows an improvement in access to safe water in the past several decades, but the forecast of increase of population numbers overcomes the impressive advances in furnishing supplies. The annual water use in the world increased from about 1,000 cubic kilometers in 1940 to 4,000 in 1990. But the increase in water use about paralleled the increase in population.

It is important to note how human use of water involves issues of health. More water is required for sanitation than for drinking and cooking. Of course, American water use is profligate compared with societies without such easy access to good water, but as shown earlier, the use of water in toilets is 9 times the amount used for cooking and drinking, and bathing is 7 times that amount. Water availability is highly correlated with the health of a poplulation. In Figure 59 it can be seen that worldwide, about 1.7 billion people lack access to sanitation, and the number of people deprived is expected to increase sharply, especially in urban areas.

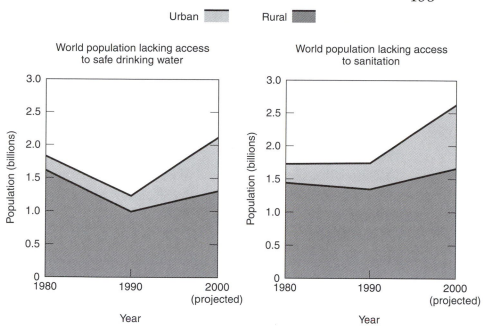

Figure 59 Safe drinking water availability has changed through time and has been increasing since 1990. However, population growth has erased any substantial gain in access to sanitation. (Adapted from Population Action International, 1993.)

Figure 60 shows, in two graphs, the population country by country having access to safe drinking water. In the United States, 99 percent of the people have such access; in Mexico and Ethiopia, the numbers are 70 and 20 percent, respectively. The second diagram of Figure 60 shows that the number of deaths of children under 5 years of age is closely associated with the access to safe drinking water.

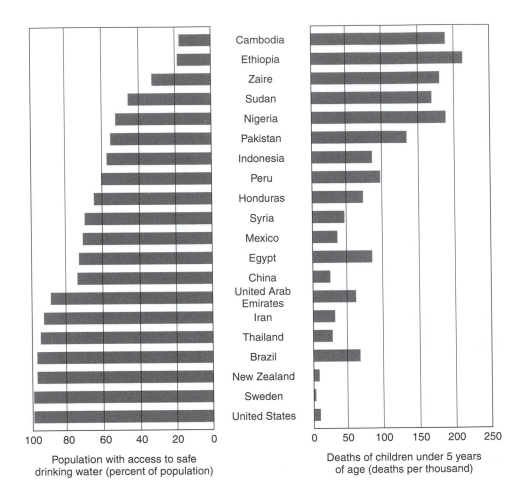

Figure 60 The population with access to safe drinking water varies from country to country; the availability of safe drinking water is inversely correlated with the death rate of small children. (Adapted from Population Action International, 1993.)

Land Management and Its Relation to Water

Water management in the United States has been less than successful. The reasons include the sharp difference of desires pitting agriculture against urban users; they include the use of rivers for power and irrigation that conflict with needs of fish and recreation; the fact that laws governing groundwater often do not reflect hydrologic realities, and the difficulty of determining and enforcing the ownership of groundwater; the fact that flood damage has increased year by year, and damageable values in flood-prone areas keep increasing; the fact that zoning and other controls of land use for general or societal good are weak and often unpopular.

Effects of dams

In the discussion of irrigation, the idea was introduced that the construction of dams has important adverse effects not usually recognized. These disadvantages were probably brought to the public mind in the widespred concern over the precipitous decline in anadromous fishes that range along the Pacific Coast from California to Alaska. Several species migrate upstream into perennial streams to spawn; the migration is blocked by dams. Fish ladders to lead migrants over a dam are not as effective as had once been hoped. In California many smolts are killed in the great pumps that move water from the Sacramento River system to the big canals and thence to cities and agriculture in the south. The pumps are located at low dams that also block fish passage. Indeed, when the pumps are operating the direction of flow is locally reversed.

155

The prevention of fish migration, though high in the public mind, tends to overshadow other important effects. The release schedules of water from dams is a major effect that takes two forms. At some dams it is the practice to release stored water at a high and constant rate for many weeks during the irrigation season. It has been stated earlier that the morphology of the river channel can be maintained only if the natural highs and lows of flow rate are the norm. The channel has been formed and maintained by flow variations, not by steady flows.

An unnatural release schedule alters the sediment movement in a channel. The Colorado River was impacted by releases from Glen Canyon Dam for years, because priority was given to maximizing power production. The releases through the power plant were dictated by the demand for peaking power which led to extreme variation in flow, hour by hour. Changes in river stage were several meters per hour. The negative results were of two kinds. The sandbars that under original conditions provided a stable community of vegetation and fauna were being eroded away, and in many cases, quite destroyed by the violent variation in flow.

Loss of the sand bars and the rapid variation in discharge took a toll on recreational boating, a sport that has become a big business. The river stage variations were an anathema to recreationists and the sandbars used as camping places were being destroyed. The flow variation became so severe a problem that detailed studies were ordered, aimed at evaluating the dam's effects. The studies sought appropriate release schedules that struck a balance between power requirements, morphological stability, and recreational needs.

Another societal loss not measurable in dollars is the destruction of scenic canyons that have aesthetic, historical, cultural, and archaeological values. The flooding of Glen Canyon of the Colorado River is considered a major cultural loss to the nation, just as the potential flooding of the Three Gorges of the Yangtze in China will be. The flooded Glen Canyon is shown in Figure 61.

Dams have resulted in the flooding of thousands of hectares of land, including cities and prime land for agriculture. They have dislocated whole populations. The building of the Three Gorges Dam on the Yangtze in China will require the resettlement of more than a million farmers and villagers. The Aswan Dam in Egypt has provided benefits to some farmers and has been a major source of electric power, but the water has covered priceless archaeological sites, destroyed ecosystems and fishing grounds, eroded banks, and altered nutrient and sediment balances. It has led to changes in the Nile Delta because the normal silt load deposited on the delta has stopped.

Figure 61 Drowning of the gorge of Glen Canyon in the Colorado River system by the construction of the Glen Canyon dam has had both beneficial and highly detrimental effects. Located in an arid climate where summer temperatures often exceed 38° C, evaporation loss is very high.

According to World Watch, before the Aswan Dam was contructed, 32 billion cubic meters of Nile water reached the Mediterranean, an amount equal to 38 percent of the average flow. Today the amount of fresh water from the Nile reaching the sea is 1.8 billion cubic meters, and the government is planning to reduce this still further. The end result will be that about one half of 1 percent of the water will flow to the sea.

One result of this change has been a decimation of commercial fishing. There were 47 species of fish in the Nile that were harvested before the dam was constructed; now only 17 species remain. The annual sardine catch has dropped by 83 percent. World Watch also notes that 15 to 19 percent of habitable land in the delta could be gone within 60 years due to subsidence resulting from lack of sediment deposition. This could displace 15 percent of the population of Egypt which is expected to reach about 100 million people. The economic effects are obviously very serious. The matter can become even more complicated if Ethiopia and Sudan increase their take from the Nile.

At present only four large reservoirs have been created in the Brazilian Amazonia, but another 75 are planned. The devastation these projects wreak on the native populations is well known. World Rivers Review cites the work of the Brazilian National Institute for Research in Amazonia that found that millions of tons of methane and carbon dioxide are emitted to the atmosphere from uncleared rainforest in tropical reservoirs. Barbina Dam in Brazil flooded 3100 square kilometers of uncleared rainforest and the rotting vegetation has polluted the reservoir water to the extent that it is unfit for drinking. The builders did not clear the forest from the reservoir area, but merely flooded it to save money.

A news item reported by Reuters discussed the Farakka Barrage built in India on the Ganges, 20 kilometers from the border with Bangladesh. The dam obstructs Ganges flow with the result that there has been gradual desertification affecting 40 million people in Bangladesh. The local people say that the dam holds back water in the dry season and floods them during the monsoon season when it releases water.

Not mentioned above is the obvious fact that reservoirs have a limited life because they gradually fill with sediment. Large reservoirs have a life that extends over several generations, so far into the future that present planning takes but little heed to the final results. However, the storage of sediment, depriving the channel downstream of the usual load, will have immediate and far-reaching consequences. When clear water is released into a channel that was formed and maintained by water heavily loaded with sediment, the channel will react, usually by downcutting. Low diversions downstream will be left high and dry and the ability to divert water will be highly compromised. Such changes below the Three Gorges Dam in China will be difficult to forecast but certainly devastating.

Even small dams built for power or irrigation have adverse impacts. If all the water is taken from a stream, diverted into a canal or penstock leading to a generator or to irrigated land, there is an unfortunate drying up of a reach of river. Some desiccated reaches are several kilometers long, ruining the fishery, causing vegetative encroachment of the channel, and foreclosing any recreational potential.

It is hard to appreciate the ubiquity of these problems until one sees the sheer number of dams on rivers of the world. International Rivers Network is deeply engaged in seeking information about dams in various countries and giving guidance and moral support to local people who are affected by dams. This organization notes that 77 percent of the water in the 139 largest rivers of the world have been significantly affected by dams and diversions, with drastic effects on ecosystems. This organization campaigns to limit the number of dams and their detrimental effects.

The Interior Columbia Basin Ecosystem Management Project has compiled data on existing dams in the interior basin of the Columbia River in Washington and Idaho. The area is only part of the basin of the Columbia but comprises about 466,000 square kilometers. In this restricted area they located at least 2,972 dams of which 1,239 have a storage capacity in excess of 61,000 cubic meters (50 acre feet).

The Water Encyclopedia showed that in 1984 there were 34,700 world dams exceeding 15 meters in height. Even in 1956 the U.S. Geological Survey reported that in the United States there were 1267 large reservoirs excluding those built just for flood control. Recognition of the mounting side effects of reservoirs has resulted in a near moratorium on dam building in the United States.

Finally, the damming of rivers tears at the fabric of a spiritual attachment humans have for rivers. This bonding is seen in the mythologies of different races, creeds and environments. Herodotus spoke of the Persian reverence for rivers. Nearly every city in Greece had a local river god. Similar feelings are expressed in the songs and tales of the original inhabitants of early America. It certainly exists in India and in all the Buddhist culture. In this regard, dams are an affront to the feeling of close association that people have for free flowing streams. There is an aesthetic aspect to this feeling of association that can be seen in art and in modern photography.

As a majority of citizens have expressed an interest in environmental quality, these basic feelings of kinship to natural rivers must be taken seriously.

Flood control

An understanding of how floodplains are formed should make it obvious that a river channel is not large enough to contain all the water produced by a drainage basin in times of heavy precipitation. To flood, that is to discharge in excess of channel capacity, is a natural characteristic of rivers. Thus the floodplain is an active part of the river during times of exceptional discharge.

Floodplains are particularly valuable to man because their soils are generally fertile and because such areas are flat and easy to use. For example, the flat terrain makes the floodplain a good place to build railroad lines, highways, warehouses, and storage areas. Proximity to a river is often convenient if boats or barges are used for transport.

If there were not some particular advantage, it would seem foolish indeed for people to establish communities on floodplains. Generally they do so because they cannot visualize the risk, even when warned of it. Then, one day the river floods, and most people who are in the way of the river suddenly wish they lived or worked up on a hill. But by that time it is too late; they own a house or other property on the floodplain and cannot afford to move. People whose work makes it particularly advantageous to be on the floodplain should realize that these advantages are obtained at the risk of flood damage.

The great flood of 1993 in the Missouri and upper Mississippi River basins caused extreme damage to property, loss of lives, disruption of business, and human suffering. The damage to property is estimated at more than $15 billion. Large areas were covered with sand derived from the failed levees, and 60 percent of the cropland in the floodplain of the Missouri River was damaged by sand deposits and scouring. More than 70,000 persons were left homeless.

There followed an effort of federal and state governments to reassess the nation's flood programs and approach to the flood problem. It is clear from this effort that there has been a major change in the perception of the problem during the past 60 years. The change in attitude has been sufficiently marked that a sketch of the history is needed. The federal involvement in flood control was documented in my earlier book, The Flood Control Controversy. For present purposes a more succinct statement will suffice.

The Corps of Engineers had both studied and done work in harbors and in navigation, but its first federal flood control works were built in 1928 on the Mississippi River. The authorization to engage in works just for flood control came after a major flood in 1927 which brought into focus the fact that some catastrophes are so great that the local entity, city, county, or water district could not bear the costs alone. There is a federal, public responsibility to help local areas with problems caused by natural events of great magnitude.

The relation to catastrophic events became somewhat tempered even in the landmark 1936 Flood Contol Act, for it included two precepts that may be summarized in the following:

- Flood control is a proper federal function and the federal government should improve or participate in the improvement if the benefits to whomsoever they may accrue are in excess of the estimated costs.

- A flood control program is justified if the lives and social security of people are adversely affected by flooding.

In subsequent years, the Acts of 1938, 1944, and others dropped the requirement of a catastrophic event. The national interests were progressively watered down and practically abandoned. Federal money covered all costs of projects except for easements, rights of way, and maintenance costs. Even then the nonfederal costs were restricted in the 1938 Act to local flood protection works, whereas reservoirs were built entirely at federal expense.

The policy became even more convoluted when it was argued by the Department of Agriculture that 75 percent of the total average annual floodwater and sediment damage occurred in small upstream tributaries. This then put Agriculture in the flood control business. However, these upstream damages are not necessarily flood damages, for gully and sheet erosion together comprise 69 percent of the total damage claimed. So inundation damage represented only a small part of the "flood damage" claimed.

Another major problem arose from the wording of the law that the benefits should exceed the cost. But the benefits that are included primarily flow from the measured value of land protected by the levees, or from flood peak reduction due to reservoir storage. Thus the program was primarily land enhancement, not flood control. The law encouraged development on the floodplain and the result, indeed, increased the flood-at-risk uses on the flood-prone area. Further, the costs enumerated did not include, or greatly undervalued, damage to the environment such as destruction of wetlands, withdrawal of floodplain land from its natural purpose of providing flood storage, reduction of groundwater recharge, harm to fish, wildlife, and aesthetic amenities.

Despite massive expenditures, flood damage increased each year. Average annual damages for the country as a whole are on the order of $2 billion to $6 billion (in 1985 dollars).

The Flood Insurance Act of 1968 changed the policy from dependence on structural means to reduce and confine flood peaks to the provision of subsidized disaster relief to individuals and communities after a flood event. The Act offered federal assistance to help flood-prone communities delineate hazard zones and offered flood insurance to floodplain occupants. The communities agreed to limit new developments on at risk properties. Flood-prone areas were mapped and the zone of hazard was chosen as that area potentially covered by a flood having a probability of 0.01, that is, a one chance in 100, the so-called 100 year event.

A rather surprising result was that far fewer people took advantage of the subsidized insurance than had been expected. Gilbert White and his associates say that the failure of floodplain dwellers to purchase insurance stems from the belief that a damaging flood will not occur during their occupancy. That idea is reinforced by the belief that if a serious flood does occur they will receive generous disaster relief if they suffer damage.

After the 1993 Missouri flood, the interagency studies developed a general plan for floodplain management. Its two goals were:

- To reduce vulnerabilty of all Americans to the danger and damage of floods.

- To preserve and enhance the natural values of the nation's floodplains.

It is obvious that federal policy changed with time in part because the hoped-for result of decreased flood damage did not materialize. There is now an emphasis on floodplain management. This involves a variety of actions. These include more effective zoning with restraints on development of flood-prone areas; widespread participation in flood insurance programs; flood proofing of selected facilities on which a public depends, such as water treatment plants and sewage disposal installations; return of portions of the floodplain to overflow areas in flood periods; integration of flood damage reduction into broader state and community development processes; use of nonstructural elements in flood control plans; coordination of federal investment with state and local management plans; inprovement of data collection networks including streamflow and damage data; promotion of hydraulic and economic studies of various approaches to damage reduction.

Though important advances have been made, the programs have not yielded their full potential. The number of families nation-wide living in flood-prone ares is estimated at 9 to 11 million, but only approximately 2.5 million flood insurance policies are in force.

Initial identification of flood hazards has been completed in over 18,200 communities, and 16,400 have adopted some kind of management measures. Also, flood insurance is no longer subsidized for new construction on a floodplain. The Federal Emergency Management Agency (FEMA) estimates that since 1975, when the insurance program was initiated, more than 2 million new buildings have been constructed out of reach of the one-percent flood; this represents an average annual reduction of $569 million in damages that would have occurred if construction had been at lower elevations.

There needs to be a greater incentive for insurance agents to recommend and sell flood insurance, and for banks to be responsible for costs of uninsured homes for which insurance has been required. There is a need also for communities to adopt and enforce building codes and land use regulations that go beyond the minimum requirements of the flood insurance program, because there is still a risk to properties that are above the level of the so-called 100 year flood.

Another aspect of the integrated planning for flood control is the possible use of floodplain land now in agriculture for channel storage during a flood. It has been proposed that there be a program of purchasing easements from flooplain owners that would allow flooding of their land under circumstances of unusual discharge. The payment of easements before floods would take the place of the present disaster relief. The amount of flood peak reduction and its monetary value have not been explored in sufficient detail to determine under what circumstances such a program would be useful.

While floodplain management has assumed a major part of damage reduction strategy, the usual and dominant structural solutions continue to be recommended by the Corps of Engineers and by county flood control districts. These solutions include dams for flood water storage, river straightening for increased channel capacity, levees for prevention of floodplain overflow, and trapezoidal concrete flumes for confinement of floodwaters.

Floodwater storage by reservoir action is designed to reduce peak discharge downstream. The volume contributed by high discharge is temporarily stored in a reservoir and released later at an acceptable discharge rate. Flood control by dams is highly effective for areas immediately downstream from the dam, but the effect on peak reduction decreases with distance below the reservoir. There are two reasons for this decrease. First, the storage in the channel itself will decrease the flood peak downstream so the effect of the dam in muted. Second, the river channel increases in capacity downstream and so the tendency to overflow also decreases.

As an example, the large channel capacity of the Mississippi River below the mouth of the Ohio River accommodated the high discharge of the river in the 1993 flood, so that the combined discharge of the main river and the Ohio was conveyed without serious flood problems.

In the central reaches of the Missouri River are two very large reservoirs, Fort Peck and Garrison. Their influence on the floods downstream in the Missouri and Mississippi was minimal. The exact effect is not easy to compute because of the many levee breaks, but the effect of those great storage reservoirs did not prevent the immense damage that occurred downstream.

Of course the structural work in the name of flood control has been useful. Levee construction is a major type of such work. The Corps of Engineers has built 17,000 km of levees and flood walls, yet FEMA estimates that about one third of the flood disasters in the United States are caused by levee overtopping or failure.

The floodplain of the Ganges in India is much wider than that of the Mississippi. Many small villages are situated on the broad expanse of flood-prone land and at least some of then are locally surrounded by a levee, just high enough to keep floodwater from inundating the housing and town center. This kind of local floodproofing might well be used on the broad floodplains of American rivers. A few homes near the Mississippi do have such protection but it is not a common practice. Indeed, during the 1993 flood it became clear that some public facilities on which the whole city depends should have had such local protection.

The effectiveness and constructive results of the operation of flood control works, especially storage in reservoirs, is undoubted. Even as early as 1951 the Corps of Engineers estimated that their works had prevented $300 million in damage annually. Of this, 60 percent of the damage prevented would have been in urban and industrial areas and 40 percent in agricultural land.

Though floodplain management is the implemented policy approach to flood damage reduction, federal, state, and county governments continue to plan and implement river straightening, concrete waterways, revetted channels, and lines of wire-encased rock gabions as the solution to local problems. The physical constraints of river channels usually have unforeseen detrimental effects. Working against natural tendencies is often unproductive in the long run. River straightening has been inflicted on about 16,000 km of channel in the United States, with dubious gains and many unforeseen losses. The ubiquity of the meandering form of rivers should urge engineers to pause before imposing an artificial pattern on a channel system.

Straightening usually takes one of two forms: a) cutting off meander loops, or b) channelization, that is, confining the river in a deep cut to prevent overflow.

Of the first type, the Mississippi experience is instructive. Navigation on the big river has at times been hampered by the natural tendency for the riffle or shallow reaches between bends to fill or deposit at high discharge. With the hope of deepening such a reach, a neck between meander curves is cut off, shortening the river reach and thereby increasing slope and, thus, scour. Winkley states that between 1930 and 1950, construction of cutoffs between Cairo and Red River Landing shortened the total length of the river 329 km. The river has reacted by increasing its length by 144 km, so the net result of the attempts at shortening was a mere half of the effort expended. The river regained length by increasing radius of curvature of the bends from 2.9 km to 3.6 km, and increasing channel width from 1.8 km to as much as 3.0 km. Meander lengths have increased from 12 km to some 16 km and the dredging to maintain navigation has skyrocketed.

Elimination of a meandering course by digging a straight deep channel to confine the river has been justified by the supposed promise of elimination of overbank flow. The potential gains of such activities are usually overwhelmed by losses resulting from channel bed erosion, undercutting and destruction of bridges, uncontrolled bank erosion, and devastation of the biotic fauna and aesthetic values.

An example studied by Emerson was the effect of channelization of the Blackwater River, Missouri. Meanders were cut off with the result that the river deepened progressively for 60 years. Bridges were undermined and three generations of bridges have been destroyed and rebuilt. The losses have far outweighed the anticipated benefits.

Among the most important challenges in water management is living with the natural processes of river behavior. Though some monetary advantages are purchased by river "improvement," these gains must be weighed against the perpetual cost of maintenance, the permanent loss of hydrologic integrity, and the depreciation of aesthetic value. The culture of our civil society can afford consideration that goes beyond immediate monetary gratification. The natural river deserves our reverence as well as our engineering capability.

Demands and Disposal

Water treatment

The United States public is so accustomed to the availability of pure water at the turn of a tap that no serious consideration has ever been given to what would be done if the water supply were discontinued for any length of time. Dependability of both supply and purity is the aim of public water-supply organizations. It is a tribute to engineers that 60,000 community water systems serve 200 million people, or 80 percent of the population in the United States.

To appreciate the problems of the design and construction of water-supply systems, it is necessary to be acquainted with the purposes a water supply must serve. Municipal water systems must be designed to serve much larger demands than merely the average home use of 350 liters per day per person. They must provide a constant supply for fighting fires and must also meet the demands of industries. These uses increase the daily per capita consumption to more than twice the household use.

The need for large amounts of water on demand to fight fires is an important determinant of the sizes of pipes required for a distribution system. The pipes must be able to supply the normal peak demand and the fire demand even if it coincides with the normal peak demand. Therefore, the size of pipes and the water pressure must be chosen to meet extreme conditions of flow for short periods. However, storage or volume requirements are dictated by the demand during extended periods of heavy water use, which usually occur during a dry period in midsummer.

In the United States, 80 percent of all water withdrawn for all uses is from streams and lakes; but approximately 75 percent of American cities derive water from wells. Most municipal wells are pumped with electric power. The modern pump is lowered into the well and placed near the bottom. It creates a pressure that forces the water upward to the surface. Most wells are pumped into a storage reservoir rather than directly into the distribution pipes.

Surface sources usually consist of a stream blocked by a dam that diverts water into pipes or into an aqueduct leading to a storage reservoir. Often the dam itself is high enough to provide storage in the reservoir behind it.

Some storage is always required during periods when demand exceeds the average rate of supply. Storage usually serves the additional purpose of providing necessary pressure for water distribution in the pipes. For example, a city reservoir may be located at sufficiently high elevation to provide pressure, or a water tower can be constructed that provides some storage as well as a constant pressure. Pumps are usually required to fill the storage reservoir or water tower. Once the water is up in the tower or reservoir, gravity will distribute the water through the pipes.

Very few cities have such nearly pure water available at the source that no treatment is necessary. In areas where water comes from deep wells or from a fenced and carefully protected watershed, only minimal treatment is required. This usually consists merely of chlorination; that is, the injection of small amounts of liquid chlorine or other disinfectant into the water to destroy bacteria.

Water commonly has some objectionable odor, taste, or murkiness. Odor and taste can usually be improved by aeration (spraying or trickling the water in such a way that it will be mixed with oxygen in the air). Aeration is the basis for the old saying that water flowing in a stream purifies itself. Given sufficient time and under proper conditions, water usually has enough oxygen dissolved in it to oxidize organic material. Aeration will tend to improve odor and taste but will not necessarily kill germs; so that old saying should not be considered a truthful one.

Odor, taste, and murkiness are generally improved by the processes of settling and filtering. To settle the impurities, water is run into a large tank where there is but little current and the water is quite still. A finely divided powder, alum, is introduced. The alum forms a "floc," or gelatinlike glob. Thousands of these little masses gradually settle to the bottom of the tank. Impurities stick to the gelatin and are swept out as the floc settles. Just as snowflakes float down through the air, gathering dust and impurities and carrying them to the ground, so does the alum settle out, carrying with it the solid impurities and even bacteria of the water.

The other common treatment is filtering water through a bed of sand. The sand screens out impurities like the filter paper or cloth in a coffee maker. Aeration is sometimes done by spraying water into the air but more often by letting water trickle through a bed of gravel.

Many municipal water-treatment plants use all four methods mentioned, first settling with alum, then filtering through sand, mixing with air, and finally treating by addition of chlorine. Water-treatment plants reduce the bacterial content of water, improve its taste and odor, and make it clear. Each of these characteristics is constantly being monitored in a water-treatment plant and definite standards must be met to protect the public health and to ensure acceptable quality.

However, salts dissolved in water are not affected by the ordinary treatment measures. In areas where water is in short supply it may be used more than once. Then, dissolved salts tend to become more concentrated with each reuse. Detergents, like the dissolved salts, are not taken out in the water-treatment process. During drought periods, detergents can become so concentrated that at times the tap water in cities downstream make suds or bubbles as it emerges from the faucet.

Many cities now are using water that has been discharged through the sewers of cities upstream. Modern water-treatment plants are quite capable of cleaning sewage wastes out of water and making it perfectly safe to drink. People do not like to think they are drinking such purified water, but in fact many are now doing so, and in perfect safety. The public should get used to the fact that water in many places is in such demand that it must be used more than once. This will be done in more areas as the population of the United States grows.

In most cities water is distributed through pipes made of cast iron but plastic pipes are becoming common. Pipes are large near the central water works and become progressively smaller as the system is subdivided. Street mains are generally of 10–15 cm (4 or 6 inches) in diameter. Such a size not only can carry water to all the houses but can also provide water to fire hydrants when necessary. The pipe leading to most houses is 25 mm in diameter, or occasionally 19 mm.

Pressure is required to provide a usable stream of water to a faucet. The usual pressure in the system of each house is 4.2 to 4.9 kg per sq cm (60 to 70 lbs per sq in). This high pressure is the reason that the water faucet cannot be shut off with the touch of a finger.

Treatment of sewage and wastes

Most of the water used in homes is for carrying off wastes. Less water is used for drinking, cooking, and even watering lawns than is used for washing clothes, doing dishes, bathing, flushing the toilet, and operating the sink garbage-disposal unit. Factories use water to dispose of such industrial wastes as chemicals or grease and to carry away excess heat. The cooling of steel and the condensing of steam are examples.

The three types of wastes are animal, vegetable, and mineral. Nearly all domestic or home wastes are animal or vegetable because they are derived from living matter. Detergents and many industrial wastes are mineral in origin. Animal or vegetable matter decays when it is dead and, in so doing, provides food for microscopic bacterial life, which in turn becomes food for higher organisms and so on through the food chain of living things. Wastes are offensive to sight and smell as well as dangerous to health because they provide food for harmful bacteria that can infect water supplies.

The waste water from homes and factories is carried in the sewer system. This water flows in pipes that, unlike those in the water-supply system, are not under pressure. The slope of the pipe usually allows gravity to carry the sewage downhill. The sewer network resembles a network of streams channels. The sewer pipes increase in size as more pipes join together, just as a river increases in size downstream. The pipe under a residential street in the upper part of the system may only be 15 cm in diameter, whereas the trunk sewer in a large city may measure several meters.

In the older cities the sewer system carries not only the sanitary sewage—that is, the waste from homes and factories, but also the storm water from the streets. Treatment plants thus have to handle a large amount of water during storm periods. In such circumstances, the bulk of the water is usually diverted so that it bypasses the treatment plant and flows directly to a river without treatment. This practice was generally abandoned and was followed by the construction of sewerage systems that carry the sanitary wastes in separate pipes from the storm runoff. Thus there are storm sewers and sanitary sewers. More modern construction in cities reverts to combined sewers and treating all the runoff because runoff from city streets is now not allowed to flow untreated into receiving bodies of water such as rivers or lakes.

Oxygen is the key element in the satisfactory decomposition and eventual purification of sewage. The work of oxygen in water is similar to its work in the body. Oxygen combines with substances that are comparable to fuel; oxidation thus is a burning process. The oxidation of sewage is not a direct chemical burning, however. Living organisms consume or burn the organic material of the sewage. The final result is the same as direct oxidation since the end products are stable compounds of oxygen, such as carbon dioxide and compounds of nitrogen and oxygen called nitrates.

If raw sewage is dumped into a clean swift stream, the oxygen in the water that was absorbed from the air and given off by aquatic plants will begin to decompose the sewage. But the process uses the dissolved oxygen upon which the fish and the cleanliness of the stream depend. If the sewage load is small in relation of the size of the stream, the oxidation can be completed, and the stream again restores its depleted oxygen from the air or from plants. But if the oxygen needed to decompose the sewage exceeds that in the stream, the sewage putrefies. Decay in the absence of air or oxygen leads to foul-smelling gases. The carbon and nitrogen of the sewage, instead of being linked to oxygen, combine with hydrogen and give off such gases as methane, which is the smell of the marsh, and ammonia. The sulfur in sewage forms another gas, which is the same gas that gives the odor to spoiled eggs.

Disposing of sewage by dumping it into a stream can be satisfactory, therefore, only when the stream is not overloaded. Because streamflow fluctuates greatly, there is a large variation in the amount of sewage a stream can oxidize satisfactorily. Partly for this reason, sewage loads tend to exceed the natural capacity of rivers to oxidize the wastes. This is one reason that sewage treatment is necessary.

There are various degrees of sewage treatment. In primary treatment the sewage first passes through a screen that removes such large objects as sticks and rags. The water then flows slowly through a grit chamber, where sand and silt settle out, and into a large settling tank, where finer suspended solids settle to the bottom or rise to the top. After the material is removed by settling, the water is chlorinated to kill bacteria and is discharged to the stream.

Primary treatment reduces the pollution load of sewage by approximately 35 percent. If greater reduction is required to avoid overloading the stream, then the sewage matter must be oxidized. This is called secondary treatment. In one method of secondary treatment, the sewage is slowly sprayed on a bed of coarse stones, usually 6 feet deep. The biological growths that develop on the stones catch the sewage matter and oxidize it. In another method, the sewage is inoculated with microbes that can oxidize organic material. The sewage is then passed into large tanks where it remains long enough for the microbes to break down the organic wastes.

According to the United States Council of Environmental Quality, 70 million people in the United States are not served by wastewater treatment. Some 100 million are provided with secondary sewage treatment, and an additional 65 million are served by tertiary or the best available treatment. Septic tanks are very important for they constitute the treatment of household wastes in a large population. David Todd states that 40 million persons in the United States are served by such individual systems and that as a result, 9 billion liters of partially treated sewage are discharged from residences into the ground every day. The efficacy of such systems depends on the fact that as water passes through finegrained soil material, the pathogens tend to be adsorbed on clay particles in a distance of about 100 meters.

Septic tanks are usually underground steel or concrete boxes that are made large enough to hold the water that the household will use during 1 or 2 days. The solids in suspension settle out and the organic matter decomposes in the absence of oxygen. The resulting outflow is offensive to sight and smell but is carried to porous tile drains from which it seeps into the ground. Most counties have codes that control the design and construction of the drainfields for septic tanks, providing, for example, a minimum distance from a stream. An inspection of the installation is required before the trenches are backfilled.

Troubles arise when accumulated sludge or scum that has floated to the top of the box is not removed. Such accumulations tend to plug up the pores in the soil and the waste then finds its way to the soil surface. If property lots are small and septic tanks of adjoining houses are too close together, there maybe insufficient ground area to absorb the water. This condition has been a source of trouble in many suburban housing developments.

Water power

Water was one of the first sources of power, other than the muscle of man or beast, for doing useful work. The old-time mill put water to work for grinding grain or sawing logs by directing a flow over one side of a wooden wheel, the rim of which was lined with buckets. The wheel turned because it was loaded on one side by the flowing water caught in the buckets. These old water wheels were awkward and cumbersome and could not supply large amounts of power. The modern reaction turbine was developed approximately 100 years ago when power for factories was needed. In the turbine, water flows down from a "head race" through curved vanes. The water pushes against the vanes and turns them. In high-speed turbines the vanes act like the propeller of a ship.

Until the development of electrical power, factories like the grist-mill were built along streams. A small dam was built to create a "fall" to operate the turbine that was used to run the machinery. Lowell, Massachusetts, and Paterson, New Jersey, were originally hydraulic towns (that is, towns that depended on water power). In such towns water diverted from the rivers was often carried in tiers of canals. Factories took water from one canal and discharged it into the next lower one. After electrical power became a reality, it was more efficient to generate electrical power and to carry the power to the factory by wires.

In 1940, approximately 40 percent of electric power was produced by water, and that percentage rapidly decreased to 20 percent in the 1960s and has continued to decrease as other sources of power have been developed. Although the amount produced by water power, as measured in kilowatts, has increased somewhat in the past decades, the total amount of electricity produced has increased by a much larger amount. Most of the increased demand for power has been met by generating plants that burn coal, gas, or oil.

Any river can produce power, but only at a few places can power be produced economically. These places are on the larger rivers where the flow is large and steady, and where the valley is narrow enough to make a good site for a dam. Most power sites that meet these requirements have been recognized and their potential has been appraised. There is a simple formula for calculating power: In metric units, multiply the fall in meters by the rate of flow in cubic meters per second, divide the product by 0.095, and the result is horsepower. The fall at Hoover Dam is 171 meters, the flow averages approximately 510 cubic meters per second, and the output is about 900,000 horsepower.

Waterpower is free in the sense that no fuel is used to produce it. Moreover, it does not directly consume water. From a conservation point of view, therefore, waterpower may be considered advantageous; however the development of waterpower consumes materials. In the American economy the cost of the materials, with their incident cost for labor, needed in most places to produce waterpower is greater than the cost of producing electricity by fuel power. As described in the previous section on dams, the hydropower dams on rivers have caused very adverse effects on fisheries and on the morphology of some rivers. In other parts of the world, dam construction continues apace and the very real disadvantages are not widely appreciated. The World Bank has lent large sums of money to countries throughout the world to build large dams and only recently has begun to see that this form of development is not necessarily good for the people in those countries. Problems resulting from the changed river regimen, problems of siltation, destruction of habitat, decimation of fisheries, and necessary disruption of the lives of local population are among the usual concerns.

When the production facilities are available, power by fossil fuels or atomic power can be made available. Because river flow is variable, a waterpower plant may be able to yield only a fraction of its potential capacity on demand. Undependable power is less valuable than "firm power." For this reason, reservoir storage is built to store water during periods of high flow for use when the flow is low, in an effort to "firm up" the power supply. Storage costs not only money but water in the form of evaporation. The average vertical distance traversed by water in rivers of the United States is approximately 530 meters. These falling waters, whose average flow is approximately 570,000 cubic meters per second, represent 300 million horsepower. Of this enormous amount of horsepower, engineers estimate that only approximately 100 million horsepower can be generated at practical power sites. Of this potential, only horsepower of 38 million has been developed, 25 million of this since 1930. A considerable part of this 25 million horsepower is a byproduct of major reservoirs built by the federal government for flood control and irrigation. Water released from these reservoirs can be passed through turbines to generate electric power. Production of electricity by waterpower in the United States is not likely to increase since the days of reservoir construction are essentially over. In relation to total electric power production, production by waterpower is likely to continue to decrease.

Water—Our Common Pleasure and Our Common Responsibility

Flood control, irrigation, water supply, and pollution control are examples of water projects whose merits should be hammered out in public discussion; unfortunately such discussions often proceed with cavalier disregard for the available knowledge in the field of hydrology.

Hydrologic principles are not controversial. The more that is known about hydrology, the easier it is to judge alternative proposals and to compare their benefits and costs. Sound decisions require an informed citizenry.

But beyond such details, it appears that in the next decades, water needs, along with ethnic strife and state boundary disputes, will dominate the relations among peoples and nations.

Water, like air, is a resource required by every living creature. Because it is so common, it is easy to take it for granted. But if any form of life is deprived, even temporarily, of access to water, a struggle will result. There is a need to place such common resources as water, land, and air on a higher plane of value and to assign them a kind of respect that Aldo Leopold called the land ethic, a recognition of the interdependence of all creatures and resources. No one species such as the Homo sapiens is any more deserving, any more entitled to dominate, than other species, for all are part of the total web. Water is a part of this whole, and it deserves what I called in another essay a reverence for rivers.

References

Ambrose, S. E., 1996, *Undaunted Courage: Meriwether Lewis, Thomas Jefferson, and the Opening of the American West*: Simon and Schuster, New York, 511 pp.

"American Rivers," 1996, Washington D.C., vol. 23 no. 1.

Batisse, M., 1993, *A Blue Plan for the Mediterranean People*: Valbonne, France, 31 pp.

Benson, M. A., 1962, *Factors influencing the occurrence of floods in a humid region of diverse terrain*: U.S. Geol. Survey Water Supply Paper 1580-B, 64 pp.

Center for Conservation Biology, 1995, *Riparian ecosystems*: Update, vol. 9 no. 1 p. 8.

Cooke, S. D., and Ahern, J., 1985, *Salinity issues and water development in the Green River Basin, Wyoming*: Water Res. Bull., vol. 21 no. 2 pp. 217–223.

Cooper, M. H., 1996, *World simmers over water*: San Francisco Examiner, Jan. 14, p. 48.

Dunne, T., and Black, R. D., 1970, *Partial-area contributions to storm runoff in a small New England watershed*: Water Resources Research, vol. 6 pp. 1296–1311.

Emerson, J. W., 1971, *Channelization: a case study*: "Science," vol. 173 pp. 325–326.

Engelmann, R., and Le Roy, P., 1993, *Sustaining water*: Population Action International, 56 pp.

Florida Conservation Foundation, 1993, *Guide to Florida environmental issues and information*: Water Park, Florida.

Haynes, C. Vance, Jr., 1995, *Geochronology of paleoenvironmental change, Clovis type site, Blackwater Draw, New Mexico*: "Geoarchaeology," vol. 10 no. 6 pp. 317–388.

Hoyt, W. G., and Langbein, W. B., 1955, *Floods*: Princeton University Press, 469 pp.

Interagency Floodplain Management Review Committee, 1994, *Science for floodplain management into the 21st century*: Washington D.C.

Interagency Advisory Committee on Water Data, 1982, *Guidelines for determining flood flow frequency*: U.S. Geol. Survey Office of Water Data Coordination, Bull. 17 B.

International Rivers Network, 1995, *Ignorant dam builders*: World Rivers Review, vol. 10 no.1 p. 2.

Lawrence, C. L., 1987, *Streamflow characteristics at hydrologic bench-mark stations*: U.S. Geol. Survey Circular 941, 123 pp.

Leopold, L. B., 1951, *Pleistocene climate in New Mexico*: "Amer. Jour. Sci.," vol. 249 pp. 152–168.

Leopold, L. B., 1962, *A national network of hydrologic benchmarks*: U.S. Geol. Survey Circular 460-B, 4 pp.

Leopold, L. B., 1971, *Trees and Streams*: "Jour. Theor. Biology," vol. 31 pp. 339–354.

Leopold, L. B., 1977, *A reverence for rivers*: "Geology," vol. 5 pp. 429–430.

Leopold, L. B., 1994, *A View of the River*: Harvard University Press, Cambridge, MA, 298 pp.

Leopold, L. B., and Maddock, T., 1954, *The Flood Control Controversy*: Ronald Press, New York, 278 pp.

Leopold, L. B., Wolman, M. G., and Miller, J. P., 1964, *Fluvial Processes in Geomorphology*: W. H. Freeman Co., New York, 522 pp.

National Oceanic and Atmospheric Admin., 1974, *Climates of the States*, 2 vols.: Water Information Center, Port Washington, N.Y.

Natural Hazards Research and Applications Information Center, 1994, *Action agenda for managing the nation's floodplains*: Special Publ. 25, Boulder, Colorado.

Pacific Rivers Council, 1995, *Upper Columbia Basin Report*: "Freeflow," Fall 1995, pp. 10–11.

Postel, S., 1995, *Where have all the rivers gone?*: "World Watch," vol. 8 no. 3 pp. 9–19.

Raven, P. H., Berg, L. R., and Johnson, G. B., 1995, *Environment*: Saunders College Publ., Philadelphia, PA, 557 pp.

Silver, C. S., 1960, *One earth one future*: Natl. Acad. Sci., Washington D.C.

Stine, Scott, 1994, *Droughts once dried up Sierra, scientists report*: San Francisco Examiner, Dec. 10.

Todd, D. K., 1980, *Groundwater hydrology*: John Wiley and Sons, New York, 534 pp.

Union of Concerned Scientists, 1994, *Global environmental problems, a status report*: Cambridge, MA, 6 pp.

Van Der Leeden, F., Troise, F. L., and Todd, D. K., 1990, *The Water Encyclopedia*: Lewis Press, Boca Raton, FL, 824 pp.

White, G. F., and Myers, M. F., 1994, *Coping with the flood: next phase*: Water Resources Update, Issue 95, 71 pp.

World Resources Institute, 1994, *World resources 1994–1995*: Oxford University Press, New York, 400 pp.

Index